Roman Sports and Spectacles

A Sourcebook

Roman Sports and Spectacles

A Sourcebook

ANNE MAHONEY
PERSEUS PROJECT
TUFTS UNIVERSITY

Focus Publishing
R. Pullins Company

ISBN 0-58510-009-9

Cover: Charioteers with horses, Roman mosaic. Museo Nazionale Romano, Rome, Italy. Scala/Art Resources, New York

Contents

Introduction

Every culture has its own forms of entertainment. In Rome the favorite entertainments were the great public games, called *ludi*,[1] and the similar spectacles originally put on for funerals of important people, called *munera*.[2] These performances might include plays, combat sports, or chariot races. The types of entertainment the Romans favored and the way they organized and funded their spectacles can tell us a great deal about Roman life.

This book sets out some of the most important textual sources for Roman sports and spectacles, so that readers may explore for themselves how the Romans entertained each other and what they thought of their spectacles. I have assumed no knowledge of Roman history or the Latin language. Key terms not only from sports but from Roman politics and culture are explained in a glossary and defined briefly in footnotes when they first appear; the most important have been left in Latin and appear in italics. In this introduction, I provide an overview of the subject and some historical background to help with the details of the selections.

Why do we study ancient sports? Sports and spectacles are the main components of the popular culture of a society that ruled most of the known world for hundreds of years: the Romans. Studying Roman sports and, especially, Romans' ideas about their sports gives us insight into how their society worked. Moreover, many of the issues that mattered to the Romans are still important to us today:

- Does watching violent entertainment harm or corrupt the spectator?
- Are athletes good role models? Does participation in sports build character?
- Is watching sports a good use of time for an educated or upper-class person? Or are sports and spectacles only for the lower classes?
- Should public funds be used to build sports arenas and theaters, or to pay for competitions?
- Who holds the record? Who won the most prize money? Who's the best?

[1] *Ludi* (sg. *ludus*) are public spectacles, including games and theater performances. See the glossary for more information.
[2] A *munus* (pl. *munera*) is a duty or office; the word comes to mean a gladiator show.

As you will see in the sources collected here, the Romans found their own solutions to these problems, and observing how they did so tells us something about what was important to them. Our sources include philosophical works, in which intellectuals theorize about the place of sport in society (Cicero, Seneca, Tertullian, Augustine); private letters between upper-class friends (Cicero, Pliny); and official government documents and correspondence (Pliny, inscriptions). These all give us an idea of the views of the people who ran Rome and its empire. We are fortunate, though, that we can also see what ordinary Romans cared about, from advertisements, graffiti, and tombstones written by and for them, and those make up the majority of the inscriptional sources in this book. Romans of all walks of life went to the chariot races and gladiator fights, and most people appear to have enjoyed them.

Roman sports are both similar to and different from the sporting events of the modern world. First of all, for the Romans, sports, theater, and other spectacles were all part of religious festivals. The closest analogy in contemporary American life might be the traditional Thanksgiving football game—but imagine football being played *only* on holidays, as an essential part of the observance of the day.

Next, the Romans were generally observers, not participants, and the competitors in Rome were usually slaves. This is particularly Roman, not an inevitable feature of a slave-holding society: in classical Greece, although it was also a slave society, citizens competed and exercised frequently, and slaves were forbidden to compete in the great games. One possible reason for this difference between Greece and Rome might be that Greek citizens fought in the armies of their city-states, and physical fitness was thought to contribute to military preparedness. Rome, on the other hand, had a standing army of professional soldiers. Another contributing factor is that gladiator combat is more dangerous than any of the Greek combat sports. A gladiator fight was normally expected to end with the death of one of the combatants, while in a Greek wrestling or boxing match both the winner and the loser could expect to survive the fight. In the one sport that was common to both Greek and Roman competitions, chariot racing, both societies used hired or slave drivers: the owner of a chariot would not be the one holding the reins. Perhaps we can imagine the typical ancient Roman being delighted with the idea of a sports TV network, and the typical ancient Greek being unimpressed.

Finally, whereas many contemporary sports are team competitions, Roman sports generally involved individuals. Gladiators usually fought one on one. A typical chariot race involved four drivers, each competing for himself against the other three. Yet Roman chariot racing came as close as anything in the ancient world to the team sports we know today. Each chariot belonged to one of four "factions" or colors, called Blue, Green, Red, and White. Tombstones and other monuments for charioteers always indicate what color they belonged to when they won their victories. Spectators were loyal to their colors, and might identify themselves as Blues or Greens depending on what team they rooted for. Literary sources (Petronius, Juvenal, Pliny) tell us that Romans often seemed to care more about the color or team than about the merits of the individual drivers. But whereas teams in modern American sports generally represent a city or a school, the four chariot factions never stood for anything other than themselves.

Roman sports, then, are individual performances, generally by slaves, for citizens to watch in the context of a religious festival, at which there would also be theatrical performances, animal shows, and other spectacles. Most Romans, as far as we can tell, were happy to go to these spectacles, though some intellectuals (Cicero, Pliny) said they would rather stay at home and read. Individual Romans had their favorite performers or teams, just as sports fans still do today. Sports so pervaded Roman culture that even the most serious epic poets could allude to chariots (Ennius) or describe an early equestrian event (Virgil), while lighter poets frequently wrote about spectacles and their audiences (Ovid, Juvenal, and especially Martial). We study Roman sports not only to recapture the excitement of a day of chariot racing but to see how one society dealt with the larger questions raised by the place of sport in that society.

Once we decide to study the ancient world, the most basic question is always "how do we know?" For Roman sports and spectacles, there are two broad sources of information: objects and texts. The largest and most obvious of the objects are the surviving performance areas, like the Colosseum (the Flavian Amphitheater) and the Circus Maximus in Rome and many other even better preserved venues elsewhere in the Roman world. Other relevant objects are the various artworks—mainly mosaics and sculptures—that depict chariot races, gladiators, and other arena events. As some of the source texts show, many Romans enjoyed having sports pictures in their homes. These objects sometimes supply information that is not available in the texts. For example, various texts refer to the *missilia*.[3] While it was always clear that this referred to a way for the emperor to distribute presents to spectators, the term was not clearly understood until a painting was found at Pompeii showing one in use.

Inscriptions are both object and text at once. They include graffiti, law-tablets, and commemorative monuments, especially tombstones. We even have advertisements for spectacles, buried in Pompeii by the eruption of Vesuvius in AD 79. Inscriptions are useful as sources because they were usually written to convey information, not as literature, and because we know they have survived unchanged since their original writing. Or, if there has been some later editing, it is usually obvious:

---

[3] The *missilia* is a mechanism that allows arena attendants to throw small gifts into the seats.

an example of this is the erasure of the names of particularly bad emperors after their deaths, leaving a blank patch on the stone. Laws and state monuments give the official view. Tombstones and other private monuments, advertising posters, and graffiti give us a look at ordinary citizens' values and priorities.

Most of the sources for Roman sports, however, as for classical antiquity generally, are literary texts, written in Latin or Greek between the second century BC and the fourth century AD. We have no contemporary copies of these texts; they have come down to us in hand-written copies made from 400 to 1,000 years or more after the texts were composed. Some of these works are scholarly, others are intended to persuade, and others are written only for the pleasure of the reader. In almost all cases the writers are members of the upper classes, senators or knights. Sometimes the writers were eyewitnesses to the events they describe, sometimes they are relying on previous authors, and sometimes they are relying on hearsay—and they do not always indicate which is which. To make sense of ancient sources it is necessary to pay attention to the type of writing, the distance in time between the author and the subject, and the author's general goals and biases.

Technical writing, like the *Natural History* of Pliny the Elder, and history and biography, as written by Livy, Tacitus, Suetonius, and Plutarch, are the most straightforward works to use as sources. The authors are trying to set forth the facts as they know them. Of course, they are also selecting which facts are most important and which sources for those facts are most reliable, just as historians still do today. None of these writers is afraid to express his own opinion about the behavior of the historical figures he writes about; for example, Suetonius refers to the "haughtiness and violence" of Caligula's treatment of the plebeians.

Other sources are more obviously biased. Philosophers like Seneca want to convince their readers that spectacles are a waste of time. Christian writers, including Tertullian and Augustine, are also writing to convince the reader of a strongly-held position: that spectacles not only are a waste of time, but can even be morally corrupting. We have a fair number of private letters, which naturally express the opinions of the letter-writers, some favorable to the games and some unfavorable. In this collection, these include letters between Cicero and his friends, letters from Pliny the Younger to friends, and letters between Pliny and the emperor Trajan.

Finally, there are the purely literary texts, including prose fiction by Apuleius and Petronius and poetry by a variety of authors. Some of these texts are descriptions of spectacles, for example Martial's account, in his *Book of Spectacles*, of the dedication games for the Flavian Amphitheater. Others mention gladiators or chariot-races in passing, as examples or in similes. These can be among the most valuable sources, since they indicate what every reader would have been expected to recognize and understand. Passing references in poems may not contain much detailed information, but they clearly demonstrate the importance of sport and spectacle in popular culture. Just like the advertising posters, these texts can give us a picture of what ordinary Romans cared about.

Objects and texts, then, are the main sources of our knowledge about Roman sports and spectacles. To understand these sources completely, it is useful to know something about the society that produced them. Although Roman society changed in significant ways from the founding of the city in 753 BC down to the end of the (Western) empire in the fifth century AD, many of its distinctively Roman features remained constant. The biggest change was in the form of government, from monarchy to democracy and back to monarchy. Rome was ruled by kings for the first 250 years or so, but became a democracy, called the Roman Republic, in around 510 BC. During the Republic, laws were passed and magistrates were elected by vote of the citizen body. The citizens were permanently divided into groups for voting purposes; majority vote within a group determined its vote in the election, and the candidate carrying a majority of the groups was the winner. Two consuls, the highest elected officials, served as co-rulers for a one-year term.

From the time of Julius Caesar, however, at the end of the first century BC, the government became more like a monarchy, though it continued to be called the Republic. In response to various civil disturbances, Julius Caesar was named dictator, an emergency grant of power greater than that of the consuls. The dictatorship had been used in emergencies before, always for short periods; Caesar's was extended several times, then made permanent. When his adopted son won the civil war that broke out again after Caesar's death in 44 BC, he also received extraordinary powers (and the new name "Augustus" in 27 BC), and in effect inherited the rule of the state. Thereafter there was always an emperor, though the consuls, the senate, and even occasional elections continued. Modern writers use the term "Republic" to refer to the period before the accession of Augustus, and call the later period the "Principate" or "Empire."

Roman society was always divided into classes based on property, and it was the wealthy who ran the government. The richest class consisted of senators and knights, and membership in this class was based on having property worth about 400 times the annual salary of an ordinary soldier in the legions. Senators were those who had held one of the higher public offices; these magistrates and ex-magistrates formed the senate, which was formally an advisory body but in fact had great influence over policy during the Republic. Senators were not supposed to have businesses or commercial interests. These were reserved for the knights, who were not active in politics. Below this class were the ordinary citizens, often called the plebeians or the plebs. The lowest citizen class were the freedmen, slaves who had been manumitted; they did not have all the rights of ordinary citizens, but any children born after their parents were freed were full citizens. Strictly, only men were real citizens, because only men could vote, but women could own property in their own names.

Rome always had slaves; even a small farmer outside the city might have a slave or two to help work the land. People became slaves either because they were born to slave parents or because they were captured, in war, by pirates, or by slave-traders. Some slaves were well-educated, often Greeks, who served as teachers, secretaries, and bookkeepers. Others worked as laborers. Being a gladiator was considered an intrinsically servile occupation; most gladiators were slaves. So were many charioteers, most *venatores*,[4] and some actors. That is, Roman public entertainment largely involved slaves performing for citizen audiences.

Roman civilization was not confined to Rome. As early as the third century BC Rome began to acquire territory outside the Italian peninsula (which had all effectively come under Roman rule in the fourth century). By the beginning of the empire, Rome ruled the entire Mediterranean coast. The area outside Italy was divided into several provinces, each administered by a governor sent from Rome, ideally an ex-consul. Provinces and towns had their own magistrates and their own budgets. They also had their own amphitheaters, festivals, and *ludi*, as some of our sources show. On the other hand, in Greece and the areas settled or influenced by Greeks, Greek culture continued alongside Roman. In particular, the Olympian, Pythian, Nemean, and Isthmian games, Greek athletic festivals founded between the eighth and the sixth centuries BC, continued to be held even as Roman-style *ludi* were also introduced.

The Roman *ludi* were always part of religious festivals (as, in fact, were the Greek games). Public officials would be responsible for organizing and funding the spectacles as part of the religious celebration. During the Republic, putting on particularly good games was a way to gain popular favor and, with luck, more votes in one's next election campaign. There were several recurring festivals, held on the same dates every year. *Ludi* could also be celebrated for special occasions, generally for victories in war; a general might make a vow to the gods that if granted victory, he would celebrate with sacrifices and *ludi*. *Ludi* generally included chariot races (*ludi circenses*, circus *ludi*) and theatrical performances (*ludi scaenici*, theatrical *ludi*), and they might include Greek-style athletic events such as boxing or foot races. Sometimes wild animals were displayed, especially at *ludi* in celebration of a foreign conquest. *Ludi* did not include gladiator combats.

Gladiators fought in *munera*, which were originally part of the ceremonies surrounding a funeral. The Latin word *munus* means a gift

---

[4] A *venator* is a hunter, especially one who hunts at a *venatio*, a wild-animal hunt staged in the arena as a spectacle.

or an obligation, and the idea was apparently that the death of a slave was owed to the dead person or to the gods of the underworld. Although funerals might also include theatrical *ludi*, these were not considered part of the *munus*. Officially, *munera* were always commemorative, but towards the end of the Republic the direct connection with a funeral began to be weakened. By the time of the Empire, gladiator combats were associated with other kinds of spectacles: wild animal displays, animal hunts in the arena, combats between animals or between people and animals; staged battles, on land or on sea; and public executions, often staged as the enactment of a story from myth or history. All of these took place in amphitheaters, except the naval battles which were more often held on artificial lakes. A typical day at the amphitheater might involve animal combats or a hunt (*venatio*) in the morning, executions at noontime, and gladiator combats in the afternoon.

The major *ludi* in the Roman calendar at the end of the Republic were:

- · the Megalensia, 4-10 April, founded in 204 BC;
- · the Cerealia or games of Ceres, 12-19 April, founded in 202 BC;
- · the Floralia, 27 April to 3 May, founded in 173 BC;
- · the games of Apollo, 6-13 July, founded in 212 BC;
- · the Roman *ludi*, 4-19 September, founded before 366 BC; and
- · the Plebeian *ludi*, 4-17 November, founded around 220 BC.

There were also other, less important annual *ludi*. The lengths of the festivals tended to increase; many of these festivals were only two or three days long when first held. At the end of the Republic, there were at least 80 days of festivals in the year, and during the Empire there were often more.[5]

Romans were generally spectators rather than participants in their spectacles. Gladiators were almost always slaves; chariot drivers and actors might be either slaves or free citizens of low status. Knights and senators were not supposed to become performers, although some did. Gladiators belonged to a troupe called a *familia* or "family," owned by a *lanista*. They fought for prize money, but the most important prize was to survive the fight. Charioteers had their own *familiae*, loosely affiliated with four "factions" or colors, called the Blue, Green, White, and Red factions. A typical race included one driver from each color racing against each other; sometimes there were two or three chariots from each color, or two colors would pair up against the other two. Drivers raced for prize money and prided themselves on winning races with large purses.

---

[5] This is not quite as many days off as it sounds, however. The Romans did not have weekends as we do. A modern worker who works five days a week and gets ten paid holidays will have 114 days off in the year.

A large purse for a chariot race was 30,000 sesterces; to hire a gladiator from his *lanista* for a fight might cost 5,000 to 15,000 sesterces. For comparison, at the beginning of the Empire, under the reign of Augustus, an ordinary soldier in the Roman army earned 900 sesterces a year. An unskilled laborer in Rome at the same period might earn 3 sesterces a day. It is always misleading to try to convert ancient money into modern terms, since the relative prices of different goods have changed; I have therefore left the money figures in the sources in terms of sesterces.

The sources collected here focus on Rome from the second century BC to the second century AD, although a few earlier and later texts are included. Greek athletics and the Greek festivals are generally ignored except where they are directly relevant to Roman practice or Roman politics. I have also ignored the later development of Roman circus *ludi* in the Byzantine empire. To make the translations more accessible and more readable, I have often interpreted allusions or inserted glosses. Technical terms have been retained in Latin and those that have not become English words are italicized: thus *ludus*, but not *gladiator*. Selections are grouped into chapters by themes; within each chapter, the selections are ordered chronologically. Connoisseurs of source-books will observe that these selections are fuller than is the practice in many such texts. For example, I have included some complete letters of Cicero rather than extracting only the paragraphs that pertain directly to sports and spectacles. This is deliberate; the context in which the Romans discussed their sports tells us something about the importance of sport relative to other facets of Roman life.

It is my pleasure to acknowledge the help and support of mentors and colleagues, Stephen Esposito, Jeffrey Henderson, Ann Vasaly, Valerie Warrior, and Jacqueline Carlon. For Focus, Albert Keith Whitaker and Jason Urbanus provided many useful suggestions. I am also grateful to the students for whom many of these translations were originally written; their pleasure in the material increased my own.

Boston, 1 July 2000

Chapter 1

Origins and Foundations

These selections describe the origins of the major *ludi* and the gradual evolution of the rules and customs associated with *ludi* and *munera*. Some of the information is historical and some is conjectural. We do know that all the major festivals were founded during the early Republic, most of them during the third century BC. Most of the information in this chapter comes from Livy, a historian spanning the first century BC and first century AD who had access to sources that are now lost to us. He wrote a history of Rome in 142 volumes, 35 of which still exist; the rest have been lost, but we have summaries of what they said.

Note how many of the early *ludi* are held in honor of the gods, usually in fulfillment of a vow. Roman sports were never pure entertainment done for their own sake but always part of a religious observance. Tertullian therefore disapproves of them: he is a Christian and finds Roman religion offensive. His book *On Spectacles* describes the Roman spectacles of his day (the second century AD) and why Christians should not watch them. He appears to be making an honest effort to discover the origins of these festivals, since he quotes various sources who give competing accounts, but his disapproval of "pagan idolatry" comes through clearly in almost every sentence.

Livy, 1.35

This excerpt describes the origins of the *ludi Romani* in the sixth century BC.

First Tarquinius[6] waged war on the Latins and captured the town of Apiolae. Because he brought back more plunder than expected from what had seemed like a small war, he put on more extravagant *ludi* than previous kings had done. It was then that the place now called the Circus Maximus was marked out. There were separate sections of seats for senators and knights to watch from, with benches on supports as much as twelve feet off the ground. There were horse races and boxers brought in from Etruria. These games are still held annually, and called the *ludi Romani* or the Great *ludi*.

---

[6] Tarquinius Priscus was the fifth king of Rome, in the sixth century BC.

5.19, 5.31, 5.49-50

The next major festival to be founded was the Capitoline *ludi*. Marcus Furius Camillus led the Romans during their conflict with the Gauls in the 390s BC. When the Gauls attacked the city, the Romans considered moving to Veii, a nearby city they had only recently conquered. Camillus insisted that Romans belonged at Rome.

5.19 (396 BC): As the dictator Camillus was giving thanks before the Senate, and everything was all ready for the coming war, he vowed that he would put on great *ludi* if he captured Veii and would restore and rededicate the temple of Mater Matuta[7] originally built by Servius Tullius about 250 years earlier.

5.31 (392 BC): Lucius Valerius Potitus and Marcus Manlius, later called "Capitolinus," were made consuls. These consuls held the great *ludi* that Camillus had vowed for the Veian war when he was dictator. In the same year the temple to Queen Juno,[8] vowed by the same dictator for the same war, was dedicated, and the women celebrated its dedication with great excitement.

5.49-50 (390 BC): Camillus had saved his country in war, then saved it again in peace by forbidding the migration to Veii, though the tributes strongly recommended this after the fire in the city and the people were inclined to agree. This was why he did not step down as dictator after his triumph: the Senate asked him not to leave the state in an unsettled condition.

First of all, since he was very dutiful and precise in religious matters, Camillus restored everything to do with the gods. He had the Senate resolve, first, that all the holy places that the enemy had occupied should be restored, re-surveyed, and purified according to rules the *duoviri*[9] would look up in the Sibylline books.[10] Next, the Senate resolved friendship with the people of Caere, because they had taken in the holy artifacts and priests of the Roman people, so that by their good will the Romans did not stop paying honor to the immortal gods. Finally, the Senate resolved to hold Capitoline *ludi* for Jupiter Best and Greatest because he had kept his temple and the citadel of the Roman people safe at a difficult time. Camillus the dictator was to establish a college to hold these *ludi*, chosen from those who lived in the citadel on the Capitoline hill.

7.2

Livy tells us the first theatrical *ludi* took place in 363 BC. He then goes on to

---

[7] Mater Matuta was a goddess of growth.
[8] Juno was one of the most important goddesses in Rome. As Queen Juno, she was part of the Capitoline Triad, whose other members were Jupiter and Minerva; these three divinities were considered the protectors of the Roman state.
[9] A *duovir* (pl. *duoviri*) is one of a committee of two. See the glossary for more information.
[10] The Sibylline books were ancient books of prophecy, kept by a special college of priests. The books were only opened and read when the Senate requested a consultation.

discuss the early history of the Roman theater—with a dig at its later expense and degeneracy. The Etruscan word "ister" which came into Latin as *histriones* is the ancestor of English "histrionic," meaning "theatrical."

In this year and the following (364-363 BC), when Gaius Sulpicius Peticus and Gaius Licinius Stolo were consuls, there was a plague. Nothing was done about it worthy of recollection except that for the third time since the founding of the city a divine banquet was held. When neither human plans nor divine assistance lessened the force of the disease, and the Romans were deeply discouraged from fear of the gods, among all their other attempts at calming the ire of the heavens they even instituted theatrical *ludi*. This was a new thing for a warlike people, whose spectacles up to now had been only in the circus. It was a small *ludus*, as beginnings almost always are, but it was a foreign institution.

Actors brought in from Etruria danced to a *tibicen*,[11] with no singing or imitating the motions of singing, but quite decorously in the Etruscan way. Then the young men began to imitate them, at the same time tossing off jokes in rough verses, and they matched their dancing to their voices. Once the idea was accepted, such *ludi* became frequent. Because "ister" is the Etruscan word for an actor, these performers were called *"histriones."* They would not improvise rough, irregular lines like the earlier Fescennine verses, but performed complete satires, with even the *tibicen*'s part written out in advance, and dancing to match.

Some years later, Livius Andronicus was the first to turn from these satires to writing plays with plots. He was also an actor in his own plays, as everyone was then. It is said that when he strained his voice from too many performances, he asked the audience's pardon and put a boy next to the *tibicen* to do the singing. He himself could then dance more vigorously since he was not also using his voice. From then on actors began to have someone else do the singing, leaving only the spoken dialogue for their own verses.

Later, plays turned away from this type of unrestricted joking and little by little the *ludi scaenici* became artistic. Young people left acting in plays to the *histriones* and began to make up amusing verses among themselves in the old way. From this practice came what were later called "exodia" or "after-pieces," especially in conjunction with Atellan farces. The latter are a type of play taken over from the Oscans, and the young people would not allow them to be contaminated by *histriones*. As a result it is still the rule that actors in Atellan farces are not removed from their tribes;[12] even though they are involved in *ludi* they still serve as soldiers.

---

[11] A *tibicen* is a musician who plays the *tibia*, a woodwind instrument like a recorder.
[12] To be "removed from one's tribe" originally meant to have one's Roman citizenship taken away, but long before Livy's time it came to mean only being transferred to a larger voting-group where one's vote would not count as much.

The origins of *ludi scaenici* should be explained along with the origins of other things, it seems to me, so that we may see how from a healthy and normal beginning they have grown into an insanity that even a wealthy kingdom could hardly tolerate.

9.40

Lucius Papirius was dictator in 308 BC. This incident shows how "Samnite" became a type of gladiator.

By decree of the Senate, the dictator had a triumph,[13] in which captured arms were the greatest part of the display. There was such a magnificent abundance of booty that golden shields were given to the bankers to adorn the forum, and this is said to be the origin of the custom of the aediles' decorating the forum as the images of the gods are brought in. To honor the gods, Romans used the characteristic arms of their enemies. The Campanians, from pride and hatred of the Samnites, armed the gladiators for the spectacle between the banquets in their style; the gladiators were called "Samnites."

10.47

This incident took place at the end of 292 BC. It became customary to put pictures of victory palms on gladiators' tombstones.

At the end of the year the new tribunes of the plebs[14] took office, but they were replaced by suffects after five days because of a flaw in the election. The censors Publius Cornelius Arvina and Gaius Marcius Rutulus performed a *lustrum*;[15] they counted 262,321 citizens. They were the twenty-sixth censors since the first ones, and this was the nineteenth *lustrum*. In the same year those who won crowns for valor in battle wore them at the *ludi Romani* for the first time, and for the first time palms were given to the victors in adaptation of the Greek custom. That same year, the curule aediles who gave the *ludi* also paved a road from the rock of Mars to Bavilla. Lucius Papirius held the consular elections; Quintus Fabius Gurgites, son of Maximus, and Decimus Junius Brutus Scaeva were elected, and Papirius himself was elected praetor.

Summary 16

The 16th book of Livy's history is one of the lost ones, so this summary is our main record of its contents. It is striking that the first gladiatorial *munus* was so important that not only did Livy write it into the history, but the writer of the summary retained it. The year under discussion is 264 BC.

---

[13] A triumph was an official celebration of a victory.

[14] Tribunes of the plebs were magistrates charged with protecting the plebeians, the citizens who were not nobles.

[15] A *lustrum* was a ritual purification performed every five years by the Roman censors, including a census of citizens.

It is said that the city of Carthage and the nation of Carthaginians were founded in this year. The Senate considered whether help should be sent to the Mamertines against the Carthaginians and Hieron king of Syracuse, and there was much debate between partisans of both sides. At last, Roman cavalry, fighting overseas for the first time, acquitted themselves very well. The enemy sued for peace and it was granted. The censors held a *lustrum*; the census registered 382,234 citizens. Decimus Junius Brutus gave the first gladiator *munus* in honor of his deceased father. The colony of Aesernia was founded. The affairs against the Carthaginians and the Vulsians went well.

24.43

These *ludi* took place in 214 BC; later, it became a standard part of the aediles' job to put on *ludi*.

Quintus Fabius Maximus the consul[16] held the consular elections. His son Quintus Fabius Maximus and Tiberius Sempronius Gracchus[17] were both elected even though they were away from Rome, Gracchus for the second time. The two curule aediles, Publius Sempronius Tuditanus and Gnaeus Fulvius Centumalus, became praetors, and along with them Marcus Atilius and Marcus Aemilius Lepidus. That year for the first time it is recorded that the curule aediles put on *ludi scaenici* for four days.

25.12

The Apollinarian games were founded in 212 BC. The prophecy quoted here was given by a seer called Marcius. Because one of his other prophecies had come true (about the battle of Cannae in 216, in which Hannibal defeated the Romans rather badly), the Senate were inclined to believe this one as well.

The prophecy said: "If you want to drive the enemy out of your land, Romans, and expel this curse that has come from a foreign people, I advise you vow games for Apollo,[18] to be celebrated every year for his good will. The people will give part at public expense and private citizens will supply additional money on their own. Let the praetor, who administers the law for the people and the plebs, be in charge of putting on these *ludi*. Let a board of ten make sacrifices in the Greek way against our enemies. If you do this correctly, you will always rejoice and your affairs will always improve, for the god who gently nurtures your fields will annihilate your enemies."

They spent one day on interpreting this prophecy. The next day, the Senate decreed that a board of ten men should look into the Sibylline books about *ludi* for Apollo and other divine matters. When the board

[16] This is the "Delayer" (*cunctator*) who held off Hannibal for many years.
[17] This Gracchus is an uncle of the more famous Gracchus brothers who served as tribunes of the plebs in the 130s BC.
[18] Apollo was a Greek god, imported into Roman religion as a god of healing.

made their report to the Senate, the senators decided that *ludi* should be vowed and held for Apollo, and that when the games were to be given, 4,800 sesterces and two large sacrificial victims should be given to the praetor. The Senate also decided that the board of ten should make a sacrifice in the Greek way against the enemies, with a bull and two white goats, their horns gilded, for Apollo, and a cow for Latona, its horns also gilded.

When the praetor was about to start the *ludi* in the Circus Maximus, he decreed that the people should bring small coins for Apollo, as many as they could afford. This is the origin of the *ludi Apollinares*, vowed and celebrated for victory, not for well-being as many people think. The people wore wreaths to watch, and the women prayed; there was a banquet for everyone in a public place and the day was filled with all sorts of sacred ceremonies.

29.14.10-14

This selection concerns the introduction of the Great Mother Goddess to Rome in 204 BC and the establishment of the *Megalensia* or *Ludi Megalenses* in her honor. The goddess was carried to Rome in the form of a statue or effigy.

Publius Cornelius Scipio Nasica was ordered to go with all the married women to Ostia to meet the goddess; he was to take her from her ship and hand her to the women who would carry her. When her ship reached the mouth of the river Tiber, he was rowed out to it in a boat by priests and, as he had been ordered, he received the goddess and brought her to shore. The leading woman of the state received her. Claudia Quinta was the most distinguished among them; her reputation had been questionable, they say, but as a result of this religious service she has come down to posterity as an example of virtue. The women passed the goddess from hand to hand all the way back to the city. Braziers of incense stood in front of the gates they passed through, carrying prayers that she would enter Rome willingly and favorably. They brought her to the temple of Victory on the Palatine on the fourth of April, and that day was a holiday. Crowds of people brought gifts to the goddess on the Palatine and there was a divine banquet and *ludi*, called Megalenses.

39.22

This selection indicates that the *ludi Taurii* are older than 186 BC. The "present day" for Livy is the first century AD.

The news came from Spain during the two days when the *ludi Taurii* were being held to honor the gods. After this, Marcus Fulvius held ten days of splendid *ludi*, which he had vowed for the Aetolian war.[19] Many

---

[19] The Aetolians, in Greece, had been allies of Rome, but had gone over to Antiochus the Great, king of the Seleucid Empire in the Middle East. Rome conquered the Aetolians in 189.

actors came from Greece in his honor. This was also the first time athletes had been exhibited in a spectacle at Rome, and there was a *venatio*[20] with lions and panthers. The whole festival had nearly the amount and variety of spectacles of the present day.

Tertullian, *On Spectacles*

Tertullian, a Christian writer of the second century AD, is concerned with what attitude Christians should take to Roman sports and spectacles. His book *On Spectacles* includes a description of what the spectacles were and where they came from. Tertullian had obviously researched the origins of spectacles and records information from all the authorities available to him.

Sec. 5: origins of *ludi*

Concerning the origins of spectacles, which are rather obscure and unknown to most of us, there is no other place to investigate than in pagan literature. There are many authors who have published notes on this matter. Here is what they say of the origin of *ludi*. Timaeus says Lydians came from Asia into Etruria under Tyrrhenus's leadership. He had yielded his kingdom to his brother. In Etruria, among the other rituals of their superstition, they also instituted spectacles and called them religion. From them the Romans adopted the performers, the time, and the appellation, for "*ludi*" comes from "Lydia."

But Varro interprets "*ludi*" as from "*ludus*," meaning "playing games," just as they used to call the Luperci playful (*ludius*) for the way they would run and play. He nonetheless considers this youthful play to belong to festival days, temples, and religion. Yet vocabulary is a side issue; the important issue is idolatry. When the *ludi* were generally called Liberalia, they sounded like they were in honor of Father Liber [Bacchus]. And indeed the country folk first held them in honor of Liber, to demonstrate their gratitude to him for wine, a benefaction they thought came from him.

After that were the so-called Consualia *ludi*, which were first in honor of Neptune, who is called Consus. Then Romulus held the Ecurria for equestrian Mars. The Consualia may also go back to Romulus, because he is said to have instituted them for the god of counsel, specifically the counsel of taking virgins from the Sabines to marry his soldiers. Obviously an excellent and virtuous counsel, even now considered right and just by the Romans, if not by God. This also makes a blot on the *ludi* from their origin—you should consider nothing good which had its beginning in evil. The origin of the games is in shamelessness, in violence, in hate, in a fratricidal founder, in the son of the god of war. Now there is an altar of Consus in the circus, buried underground at the first turning-post

---

[20] A *venatio* is a staged hunt.

and inscribed: "Consus mighty in counsel, Mars in war, Lares[21] in the harvest."[22] Public priests offer a sacrifice there on the nones of July [the 7th], and 12 days before the calends of September [21 August] the priest of Quirinus and the Vestal Virgins do the same. Romulus also instituted *ludi* for Jupiter Feretrius on the Tarpeian Rock, called the Tarpeian or Capitoline games according to Piso. After this Numa Pompilius made *ludi* for Mars and Robigo (their goddess of the blight or mildew on plants); and Tullus Hostilius, Ancus Martius, and the rest also had *ludi*. And in which order they came and to what idols they instituted *ludi* is all found in Suetonius Tranquillus and his sources.

Sec. 8: description of the circus

The circus is principally sacred to the Sun. There is a temple to the Sun in the center of the space and its image shines from the top of the temple, because they did not think he whom they had out in the open could be properly served under a roof. Some people say the first circus spectacle was produced by the Sun for Circe, his daughter, and they say the name "circus" comes from her name. It is clear that the sorceress did this business in the name of those whose priestess she was, that is the demons and the fallen angels. What idolatries do you recognize, then, in the nature of this place? Every ornament in the circus is a temple on its own. They attribute the eggs that mark the laps to Castor and Pollux, and they do not blush to believe that those brothers came from Jupiter as a swan. The dolphins spout for Neptune; the columns bear Sessia from sowing [*sementis*], Messia from harvesting [*messis*], and Tutulina from guarding the grain [*tutela*]. In front of them appear three altars for the triple god, Great, Powerful, and Strong. They believe these are Samothracian. As Hermateles says, the immensity of the obelisk prostitutes itself to the Sun. The writing on it comes from the same place and is an Egyptian superstition. The assembly of demons was dull without its Great Mother, so she presides from the moat. Consus, as we said [in sec. 5], has an underground altar near the turning-post. An idol also made the turning-posts, called Murcian, for they say Murcia is a goddess of love and have consecrated a temple to her there.

Sec. 9: origins of chariot racing

Now, about the skills exhibited in the circus. Once equestrianism was simple: just get on the horse's back and go. In this common usage there was no problem. But when the equestrian art was brought into the *games*, it changed from a service to God to the work of the devil. This kind of spectacle belongs to Castor and Pollux, who according to Stesichorus

---

[21] The Lares are domestic gods, in origin probably gods of the farm.
[22] The text of the inscription on the altar of Consus is unclear; what is in the text of Tertullian does not make sense.

received horses from Mercury. But Neptune, whom the Greeks call Hippios, is also equestrian. The ridden horse is sacred to Jupiter, the four-horse chariot to the Sun, and the two-horse chariot to the Moon. But:

> Erichthonius first dared to yoke four horses to his cart,
> Conqueror he stood and swift with his wheels. [Virgil, *Georgics* 3.113]

Erichthonius was the son of Minerva and Vulcan, and also of lust fallen to the ground. He is a demonic monster, not a serpent but the devil himself. If in fact Trochilus of Argos is the inventor of the chariot, he dedicated his work to Juno first of all. If Romulus showed the first four-horse chariot at Rome, I think he too is listed among the idols, if he is also Quirinus. Chariots produced by such creators, along with their drivers, are deservedly dressed in the colors[23] of idolatry. For at first there were only two, white and red. White is for winter, because of the white snow, and red was vowed to summer for the redness of the sun. Afterwards, driven as much by pleasure as by superstition, some consecrated the red to Mars, some the white to the Zephyrs, the green to Mother Earth or spring, the blue to the Sky and the Sea or to autumn. Because God condemns every form of idolatry, this form is also condemned which desecrates the elements of the world.

Sec. 12: origins of the *munus*

It remains to discuss the most famous and most popular of all spectacles. It is called a *munus* because it is a duty, which is what *"munus"* means. The ancients believed to put on this spectacle was a duty to the dead, after they had seasoned it with a more civilized cruelty. For once, because it was believed that the souls of the dead have to be appeased with human blood, at funerals they would sacrifice prisoners or slaves bought cheap for the purpose. Afterwards they preferred to cover their impiety with pleasure. So they trained the people they procured with whatever arms were available, so they would know how to be killed, and then expended them at the tomb on the day appointed for the funeral. Thus they were consoled for death by murder. This is the origin of the *munus*. But little by little they came to have as much charm as cruelty, because the festival was not good enough unless human bodies were also taken apart by wild beasts. Because it was once a sacrifice for the dead, the *munus* can be considered a funeral rite, but then it is idolatry, because worshipping the dead is a kind of idolatry. And devils live in the statues and images of the dead.

Suetonius, *Life of Julius Caesar*, sec. 26

Caesar's *munus* for his daughter Julia, who had died some years earlier, was apparently the first time anyone held a gladiatorial *munus* not immediately

---

[23] See chapter 3 and the glossary for more on the "colors" or factions of chariot drivers.

connected with a funeral. It took place after Caesar's return from Gaul, around 50 BC.

Caesar announced a *munus* in memory of his daughter, something no one had ever done before. To heighten anticipation, he provided a banquet using his own household cooks as well as hired caterers. He ordered that well-known gladiators whose fighting did not please the spectators should be removed from the amphitheater, but not put to death. He had new gladiators trained, not by *lanistae*[24] in the gladiator school, but by Roman knights who were skilled fighters and even by senators in their own homes; he wrote letters asking these knights and senators to give individual attention to their trainees.

Ovid, *Fasti* 3.809-8130

Ovid's *Fasti* is a long poem about the calendar, with sections for each important festival day or anniversary. It is unfinished; he only wrote the first six books, January through June. This section of the *Fasti* covers 19 March, the Quinquatria.

There is one day in the middle on which the rites of Minerva take place, and it takes its name from five days joined together. The first day is empty of bloodshed, and one must not contend with swords, because it is Minerva's birthday. The second and third are celebrated on the smooth sand, and the warlike goddess delights in sword-thrusts.

---

[24] *Lanistae* (sg. *lanista*) are the owners and managers of gladiator troupes.

Chapter 2

Gladiators

These selections characterize gladiators, real or stereotyped. In the selections from Lucilius, Horace, Juvenal, and Petronius, we see gladiators from a satirist's point of view. The inscriptions, on the other hand, are the tombstones and monuments of real gladiators or of the wealthy citizens who put on *munera*. From them we can see how many kinds of gladiators there were. We can also see how many other kinds of people had jobs related to gladiator *munera*: trainers, musicians, amphitheater guards and doormen. Finally, the selections from Livy and Plutarch tell the story of Spartacus, perhaps the most famous gladiator of all. Like most gladiators, he was a slave, but he became the master of his group of rebels and managed to hold off the Roman army for two years (73-71 BC). The idea that a group of runaway slaves could fight so well was threatening to the Romans, but Spartacus's courage and tenacity were also considered exemplary Roman virtues.

Lucilius, *Satires* 172-181 ROL = 149-158 Marx

This passage consists of two fragments, which were probably not consecutive in the original poem. It indicates that there were star gladiators as early as the middle of the second century BC.

There was a certain Alsernianus, a Samnite, at a *munus* given by the Flaccus family, a filthy fellow, ideally suited to such a life. He was matched with Pacideianus, far and away the best gladiator in all of history.

"Then I will kill him and I'll win, if that's what you're asking for," says Pacideianus, "and here's how I think it will be. First I'll get it in the mouth, before I get my sword into the dumbbell's stomach and his lungs. I hate the man. I'm all riled up to fight. It won't go on any longer between us than the time it takes to get a sword in our hands. That's how carried away I am by zeal, hatred, and anger against him."

Livy, *Summaries* 95-97.

In 73 BC, a gladiator called Spartacus led a revolt of gladiators from a *ludus* (gladiator school) in Capua. It took two years for the Roman army to put down the revolt. These selections come from summaries of lost books of Livy's history.

95. 74 gladiators escaped from the school of Lentulus in Capua. Crixus

and Spartacus, their leaders, gathered a large troop of slaves and debtors from the workhouse and in the ensuing battle conquered the legate[25] Claudius Pulcher and the praetor[26] Publius Varenus.

96. Quintus Arrius, the praetor, killed Crixus, the leader of the runaways, along with 20,000 men. Gnaeus Lentulus, consul,[27] fought Spartacus without success. Spartacus beat Lucius Gellius, the other consul, and Arrius in battle. Gaius Cassius, proconsul,[28] and Gnaeus Manlius, praetor, fought Spartacus without success, and the war was turned over to Marcus Crassus the praetor.

97. Marcus Crassus, praetor, at first fought successfully against the part of the runaways who were Gauls and Germans, and killed 35,000 of them including their leaders Castus and Gannicus. He then fought it out with Spartacus, and killed him with 60,000 men.

Plutarch, *Life of Crassus* 8-11

Plutarch's account of Spartacus is fuller than what remains of Livy's but not necessarily more accurate. The slave wars in Sicily that Spartacus considers reviving had ended less than 30 years earlier; this is part of the reason why Spartacus's own slave uprising was so threatening. This selection comes from a biography of Crassus, the notoriously wealthy man who later joined with Caesar and Pompey to form the "first triumvirate."

8. The uprising of gladiators and pillaging of Italy, which many people call "Spartacus's war," began for the following reasons. A man called Lentulus Batiatus had a gladiator school at Capua. Most of his gladiators were Gauls or Thracians who had been sold into slavery and made gladiators not because they had done anything wrong but because of their master's injustice. Two hundred of them planned to escape, but when they heard their plan had been betrayed, eighty-two of them broke out before the time they'd agreed on, armed with knives and skewers from the kitchen. On the road they met up with wagons carrying gladiator weapons to another city, so they appropriated them and armed themselves. When they reached a defensible location they elected three leaders, chief among whom was Spartacus, a Thracian of the Maedi people. Spartacus was brave and strong but also more intelligent and gentle than most men of his station in life, and more like a Greek than most Thracians.[29]

---

[25] A legate is a high-ranking officer of the Roman army.

[26] A praetor is a high-ranking magistrate. See the glossary for more information.

[27] The two consuls were the highest-ranking elected officials in Rome.

[28] A proconsul is someone who serves in place of a consul. Usually the term applies to a governor of a Roman province: when there were not enough ex-consuls available to manage all the provinces, proconsuls would be named to fill in.

[29] Plutarch was a Greek, not a Roman; a Roman writer might have said Spartacus was "like a Roman."

They tell the following story about Spartacus. When he was first brought into Rome to be sold, a serpent coiled itself around his face while he was asleep. A woman of the same nationality, a seer, possessed by Dionysus, said it was a sign that a great and fearsome power would lead Spartacus to an unfortunate death. This woman escaped along with him.

9. The gladiators were pursued by Capuans, whom they fought off, capturing in the process some more warlike weapons, which they were happy to have; they discarded the gladiator weapons as dishonorable and barbarous. Then Clodius, the praetor, sent from Rome with 3,000 men, besieged them in a mountain pass with only one narrow, difficult exit, at which Clodius posted guards. The rest of the area was steep and sheer, and wild vines grew on the top. The gladiators cut the most serviceable wood and wove long ladders, which they attached to the cliffs from above, and all but one got down safely. The last man stayed behind to throw down the weapons, and came down to safety himself after they were all down. The Romans did not see this, so were astonished when the gladiators suddenly surrounded them, routed them, and took over their camp. Many of the local cowherds and shepherds joined up with them, good fighters and fast runners; the gladiators gave some of them heavy arms and used some as scouts and light troops.

Next the Romans sent out Publius Varinus, another praetor. The rebels first attacked his lieutenant Furius and put his 3,000 troops to flight. Varinus's advisor and co-commander Cossinius, with a significant force, was bathing at Salinae near Pompeii when Spartacus almost captured him. He got away with great difficulty, but Spartacus seized his supplies, then followed him closely and at last took his camp, killing many men including Cossinius himself.

Spartacus met the praetor Varinus in many other battles, finally taking his lictors[30] and even his horse as prisoners. He was by now powerful and fearsome, but he was a realist and knew he could not overcome the power of Rome. He therefore began leading his army toward the Alps, thinking the best plan was to cross them and return to their home territories in Thrace and Gaul. His men, however, who felt they were a large enough army to be powerful, refused to obey and instead set to plundering Italy.

Now it was no longer just the shameful indignity of this rebellion that disturbed the Senate, but fear at the danger, so they sent out both consuls as they would to the greatest and most difficult war. One consul, Gellius, rapidly attacked the Germans, who from arrogance had set themselves apart from Spartacus's troops, and thoroughly destroyed them. Lentulus, the other consul, surrounded Spartacus with a large force, but Spartacus rushed their lines, defeated the legates, and seized all their supplies.

---

[30] Lictors were the honor guard that accompanied a Roman magistrate. Higher-ranking magistrates had more lictors.

Spartacus then pushed on for the Alps, but Cassius, governor of Cisalpine Gaul, came to meet him with 10,000 men. In the ensuing battle Cassius was defeated, lost many men, and only got away himself with difficulty.

10. When the Senate heard this, they angrily relieved the consuls of this command and put Crassus in charge of the war. Because of his reputation and his popularity, many distinguished men joined his army. Crassus stationed himself near Picenum, where Spartacus was heading. He sent his legate Mummius with two legions to follow around behind the enemy, ordering him not to engage them, not even in a small skirmish. But Mummius, as soon as he had any hope of success, joined battle and was defeated. Many of his men were killed, while others saved themselves by throwing away their arms and fleeing.

Crassus was furious with Mummius. He armed the soldiers again but insisted on pledges that they would keep these weapons. Then he took 500 of the leaders who had instigated the flight and divided them into groups of 10. He chose one man by lot from each group and executed them. This was an old traditional punishment for soldiers. It is a shameful way to die, involving horrible punishment with the entire rest of the army watching.

After imposing this correction, Crassus led his men against the enemy. Spartacus had quietly withdrawn through Lucania toward the sea. At the harbor he met up with some Cilissan pirates and started thinking about Sicily: if he sent 2,000 men to the island, he could rekindle the slave wars there, which had ended not long ago and could easily be revived. He reached an agreement with the Cilissans and gave them gifts, but they deceived him and sailed away. So he marched back from the sea and encamped on the peninsula of Rhegium. Crassus arrived and recognized from the nature of the place what had to be done: he began to build a wall across the neck of the peninsula, keeping his soldiers busy and his enemy unsupplied. It was a large, difficult task, but he accomplished it in surprisingly little time. He dug a trench across the neck from one shore to the other, 300 stades long [about 60 kilometers or 34 miles], 50 feet wide and as many feet deep. Above this trench he put a marvelously high, strong wall.

At first Spartacus paid no attention to this activity. When the booty started running out and he wanted to leave, he realized he was under siege. There was nothing he could take in the peninsula, so he waited for a stormy, snowy night, then filled in a small part of the trench with earth and branches, allowing him to bring out a third of his army.

11. Crassus was now afraid Spartacus would get the idea of attacking Rome, but he was encouraged by disagreements among the enemy. Some of them had split off and made camp near Lake Lucania, whose water, they say, changes over time: it becomes sweet, then goes back to being salty

and undrinkable. Crassus attacked this group and drove them far away from the lake, but the pursuit and slaughter were stopped by the sudden appearance of Spartacus, who kept his men from fleeing.

Crassus had earlier written to the Senate that they should recall Lucullus from Thrace and Pompey from Spain. Now he had second thoughts, and hurried to finish up the war before they arrived: he realized that the glory of the victory would go to those who came in to help, not to himself. He decided he would first attack those who had split off from Spartacus, whose leaders were Gannicus and Castus. He ordered 6,000 men to go in secret to the top of a certain hill. They were trying to avoid detection, with their helmets covered, but were seen by two women making a sacrifice in front of the enemies. They were in danger until Crassus suddenly appeared and began the fiercest battle of the war, in which 12,300 enemies perished. Afterward he found only two wounded in the back. All the others had died standing their ground and facing up to the Romans.

After this defeat, Spartacus withdrew to the mountains of Petelia. Quintus, a legate, and Scrofa, the quaestor,[31] followed close behind. Spartacus, turning around, put the Romans to flight; they barely saved themselves and the wounded quaestor. This victory destroyed Spartacus, for now the runaway slaves were over-confident. They no longer wanted to avoid battle and they did not obey their leaders, but once they started to march they surrounded the leaders and forced them to go back through Lucania and attack Crassus and the Romans.

Pompey's arrival was being announced, and in the election assemblies there were more than a few saying victory in this war was his: he would show up, fight, and finish the war. Crassus therefore was eager to fight, so encamped near the enemy. He was digging a trench when the slaves leapt out and began to fight with the workers. More and more men joined in on both sides. Spartacus, seeing what he had to do, formed his army in proper order. When his horse was brought to him he drew his sword and said, "If I win, I'll have as many of the enemies' good horses as I want. If not, I'll have no need of any." He then killed his horse. Then he made straight for Crassus himself through the flying weapons; he did not reach him but killed two centurions who attacked him.

In the end, his men fled and Spartacus stood alone, surrounded by many Romans, defending himself until he died. Crassus had been lucky and competent as general, and had put himself at risk, but nevertheless the glory of the victory went to Pompey. Pompey met some 5,000 of the rebels fleeing the battle and destroyed them. He then wrote to the Senate that Crassus had obviously scored a great victory over the runaway slaves, but he himself had cut out the roots of the war. So Pompey had a triumph

---

[31] A quaestor is a low-ranking magistrate.

for his victory over Sertorius in Spain, but Crassus did not ask for a major triumph and settled for the so-called ovation. Even this small triumph, celebrated on foot instead of in a triumphal *quadriga*,[32] seemed ignoble for a war against slaves.

Horace, *Satires* 2.3.82-89

In this excerpt, a philosophically-inclined speaker equates greed with insanity. The passage implies that the funeral *munus* could be paid for from the deceased's estate.

The very largest share of hellebore[33] should be given to greedy people; I expect we can reasonably assign them all the hellebore in Anticyra. Staberius had his heirs inscribe the size of his estate on his tombstone, or else they'd have to give a show of 100 pairs of gladiators to the people, and a banquet good enough for Arrius,[34] with as much grain as the African harvest. "Whether I desire this rightly or wrongly, don't be harsh with me": I think this shows Staberius's prudence.

Juvenal, *Satire* 3.34-37

This passage is one of the few allusions to "thumbs down" in the Roman arena, a gesture whose interpretation has changed in the centuries since Juvenal. The crowd could signal that a losing gladiator was to be spared by pointing their thumbs *down*, to signify dropping the sword. They signaled he was to be killed by turning their thumbs *up*, or towards their own chests.[35]

The one-time horn players, traveling to municipal arenas, their puffed-out cheeks known in all the little towns, are now putting on their own *munera*, and when the crowd gives the order with upturned thumb, they kill just as the people want.

Petronius, *Satyricon* sec. 29-30.

The narrator is entering Trimalchio's house for the first time. Trimalchio is a freedman with more money than class. Pictures, mosaics, and statues showing gladiators were popular decorations all over the Roman world, and quite a few have survived.

Next I saw a big cupboard in a corner. In it there were silver Lares, a marble statue of Venus, and a pretty large gold box that they told me contained the first shavings of the master's beard. So then I asked the steward what pictures they had in the middle. "The *Iliad* and the

---

[32] A *quadriga* is a four-horse chariot, the kind used in races as well as in triumphal parades.

[33] Hellebore (a plant) was considered to be a cure for insanity, and Anticyra was where it was grown.

[34] Arrius was notorious for having given a funeral dinner for several thousand guests. We do not know whether Staberius was equally notorious or whether Horace invented him for this poem.

[35] The interpretation of this passage, and of the gesture, is debated.

Odyssey," he said, "and Laenatis's gladiator *munus*." He didn't let me hang around ogling the art.

Satyricon sec. 45

This selection is from the conversation at Trimalchio's dinner party.

C'mon (said Echion, a rag-dealer), don't talk so glum. "If it isn't one thing, it's another," said the countryman who'd lost his spotted pig. What isn't there today will be tomorrow; that's how life goes. By Hercules, this country would be perfect if it only had men. It's in a bit of trouble now, but then so are other places. We shouldn't be so picky: the sky is straight up from everyplace. If you were someplace else, you'd say that here, pigs walk around already cooked. Look, we're gonna have an excellent *munus* on the third day of the festival, not just some *lanista's familia*[36] but a bunch of freedmen. Our boy Titus has a good heart (and a hot head); it'll be something real, no half-assed job. I'm like family with him and he's no wishy-washy weakling. We'll have the best sword fighting, no running away, a regular butcher-shop right there in the amphitheater. And he's got what it takes: he got 30 million *sesterces*[37] when his poor father died. So if he spent 400,000, his estate wouldn't feel it, and he'll be talked about forever. He's already got some freaks, a woman *essedarius*,[38] and Glyco's steward that got caught showing the mistress a good time. You'll see the audience brawling, the jealous husbands against the tomcats. Old penny-pinching Glyco giving his steward to the beasts—that's like him going in there himself. How is the slave at fault, if she made him do it? Better to send off that chamber-pot of a wife, let a bull toss her. But, if you can't beat the donkey, beat the saddle. How did Glyco think any twig off Hermogenes's family tree would ever come to a good end? Sharp? I'll say—that one could cut the talons off a flying hawk. A snake doesn't give birth to a rope. Oh Glyco, Glyco's the one getting punished. As long as he lives he'll bear the scar: only the God of Death can take it away. Oh well, everyone makes his own mistakes.

Anyway, smells to me like Mammaea's gonna give us a banquet, 2 *denarii*[39] for me and mine. Which if he does, he'll definitely be more popular than Norbanus. You know, he ought to sail right into office. And, really, what good has he ever done for us? He put on two-bit gladiators, already half dead, that would fall over if you blew on them: I've seen *bestiarii*[40] that were better men. The ones on horseback were like some picture off a lamp; you would have thought they were squawking chickens. One was useless as a mule's balls, the other had a limp, the one who

[36] The base meaning of *familia* is "household" or "family," but in this context it refers to a troupe of gladiators.

[37] *Sesterces* are money; see the introduction and the glossary for the approximate purchasing power of a sestertius.

[38] An *essedarius* is a gladiator who fights from a war-chariot.

[39] A *denarius* is a small unit of money.

[40] A *bestiarius* (pl. *bestiarii*) is someone who fights in the arena against animals.

came in for the second round was a walking dead body replacing the one they dragged out hamstrung. One of them had a little spirit, the *Thraex*,[41] but even he was working strictly to rule. In short, they all got beaten afterwards, especially 'cause the crowd kept yelling "Give it to them!" Definitely a pure rout. So he says "But I gave you a *munus*." Sure, Norbanus, and I applauded. Add it up: I'm giving you more than I got. One hand washes the other, you know.

Satyricon sec. 117

The narrator and his cronies, plotting a crime, swear the gladiators' oath.

"So let's stop fooling around," said Eumolpus. "Put me in charge, if you like the idea." Nobody dared complain. Then, so the lie would stay safe among us all, we all swore a solemn oath as Eumolpus told us: to be burned, bound, beaten, and put to death by the sword, and to do whatever else Eumolpus might order us. Just like real gladiators we faithfully made over our bodies and souls to our master.

Pliny the Younger, Letter 6.34

Maximus has served as a municipal official in Verona. The *munus* he intends to give will officially be a memorial to his wife, but in fact will be a party for the city. Note that even in a small town outside Rome a *munus* would include both gladiators and an animal show.

Gaius Plinius to his friend Maximus

You did well to promise a gladiatorial *munus* to our friends in Verona, since they've done well by you even though you were unhappy about the appointment at first. After all, that's where you found your wife, who was so wonderful and whom you loved so much. It's right to do something in her memory, like a spectacle and especially a big funeral. Besides, there were so many people who asked you that you couldn't keep saying no: it would have seemed harsh. It is excellent, too, that you have been so liberally generous, which also shows your great heart. I should like all those African beasts you've bought to show up on the appointed day, but it's possible that they'll be held up by a storm. You deserve to have them, but if you have less to exhibit, it is out of your hands. Farewell.

Inscriptions

ILS 5145, at Pompeii. The first three texts here are posters advertising *munera* held in the first century AD. Note that awnings, pulled over the top of the arena to shade the spectators from the sun, are an optional feature, prominently mentioned in ads if they will be used.

Decimus Lucretius Satrius Valentis, permanent *flamen*[42] of Nero Caesar

---

[41] A *Thraex* is a gladiator in Thracian armor.
[42] A *flamen* is a priest.

son of Augustus, will have 20 pairs of gladiators fight, and his son Decimus Lucretius Valentis will exhibit 20 pairs, at Pompeii 8-12 September. There will be a lawful *venatio* and awnings. Aemelius Celer wrote this.

CIL 4.1189, at Pompeii.

The gladiator *familia* of Aulus Suettius Certus the aedile will fight at Pompeii on the last day of May. There will be a *venatio* and awnings.

CIL 4.1190, at Pompeii, referring to the same *munus*

The gladiator family of Aulus Suettius Certus the aedile will fight at Pompeii on the last day of May. There will be a *venatio* and awnings. May Nero be happy in all his *munera*.

ILS 5088 = CIL 6.10194, at Rome, fragmentary tomb of a gladiator.

The "triumph" of Trajan here refers to his funeral *munus* in AD 117, at which his deification would have been announced. The stone is broken, so the inscription is not complete.

Marcus Antonius Exochus, born at Alexandria, came to Rome for the triumph of the deified Trajan. On the second day, as a novice, he fought with Caesar's slave Araxis and received *missio*;[43] at Rome in the same *munus* on the ninth day he fought Fimbria the freedman in his ninth fight and received *missio*; at Rome on the same day....

ILS 5058 = CIL 10.1211: from Campania, AD 170. A monument to a leading citizen.

To Lucius Egnatius Inventus, father of Lucius Egnatius Pollus Rufus, honored with the Public Horse by the Emperors Antoninus and Verus Augustus. When he was given permission by the Emperor to put on a *munus* with spectacles, he gave a day of gladiators entirely at his own expense. Place given by decree of the decuriones to the colony and its inhabitants on account of his generosity. Erected 21 March in the consulate of Clarus and Cetegus.

ILS 5084, 5084a = CIL 6.631, 6.632, and probably also 6.3713: near Rome, AD 177

These gladiators are presumably almost all slaves, except for those who have Roman-style double names, praenomen[44] and nomen. Note that in this organization *murmillo*[45] and *contraretiarius* are separate styles. Those listed as "examiners" are identified by the abbreviation "sp" on the inscription; we do not know for sure what it stands for. Those listed without a title probably have the same title as the preceding man. As "decuria" means a group of 10, and there are only 2 in the fourth decuria, we know we are missing some of the text.

---

[43] *Missio* is the privilege of stopping a gladiator combat before either fighter has been killed.

[44] The three parts of a Roman citizen's name were the *praenomen*, the *nomen*, and the *cognomen*. See the glossary, under *cognomen*.

[45] *Murmillo, hoplomachus*, and so on are types of gladiator, distinguished by the kind of armor and weapons they use; see the glossary for details.

In the consulate of the Emperor Caesar Lucius Aurelius Commodus and Marcus Plautius Quintillus. The leaders of the collegium of Silvanus Aurelianus, overseers Marcus Aurelius Hilarus, freedman of Augustus, and Coelius Magnus the *cryptarius*.

First decuria:

> Borysthenes, veteran Thraex
> Clonius, veteran *hoplomachus*
> Callisthenes, veteran Thraex
> Zosimus, veteran *essedarius*
> Plution, veteran *essedarius*
> Pertinax, veteran *contraretiarius*
> Carpophorus, veteran *murmillo*
> Crispinus, veteran *murmillo*
> Pardus, veteran *provocator*
> Miletus, veteran *murmillo*

Second decuria:

> Vitulus, veteran *murmillo*
> Demosthenes, *manicarius*
> Felicianus, novice *retiarius*
> Servandus, novice *retiarius*
> Iuvenus, examiner of *murmillones*
> Ripanus, novice *contraretiarius*
> Silvanus, novice *contraretiarius*
> Secundinus, novice *provocator*
> Eluther, novice Thraex
> Pirata, *unctor*

Third decuria:

> Barosus, novice *contraretiarius*
> Aemelianus, *contraretiarius*
> Ulpius Euporas
> Proshodus, novice *contraretiarius*
> Aurelius Felicianus
> Aurelius Felix
> Zoilus, *paganus*
> Flavius Mariscus
> Flavius Sanctus
> Diodorus, *paganus*

Fourth decuria:

> Aprilis, *paegniarius*
> Zosimus, examiner of Thraeces

All happiness to the Emperor! May the *familia* of Salvus Commodus be happy! The *familia* restored (this statue of?) Silvanus Augustus. Severianus Maximus, procurator, dedicated this. May the order of leaders be happy, and the learned trainers, under the care of Marcus Aurelius Euporan, freedman of Augustus. Severianus Maximus Commodianus, may Caesar be gracious to you.

ILS 5062 = CIL 10.6012: from Minturno, AD 249. It was unusual for every pair of gladiators in a *munus* to fight to the death; more often some pairs would receive *missio*.

To Publius Baebius Terentius Justus, son of Publius. His peers have decided to erect a statue to this most excellent man because he has held every office in the town, because he has always shown equal respect for individuals and the city as a whole, and because after his term as *duovir* he gave the people a most excellent gladiatorial *munus*, with a procession, and by the indulgence of the Emperor willingly showed 3 pairs with beasts and herbivores. On the occasion of the dedication of this statue he gave 3 *denarii* to each of the decuriones. At Minturno over 4 days he put on 11 pairs, of whom he killed[46] 11 first-rate gladiators from Campania, and also cruelly killed 10 bears. As you remember, good citizens, he killed 4 herbivores of all kinds on each day. Dedicated 1 August in the consulate of Aemilianus (for the second time) and Aquilinus.

ILS 5083 = CIL 9.465: from Venusia. Gladiators not identified as slaves are free citizens, *auctorati*. The stone is broken, so an indication of a date may have been lost.

The gladiator *familia* of Gaius Salvius Capito
Mounted fighters: Mandatus, Rabirius's slave, 3 victories, 2 crowns.[47]
Thraeces: Secundus, Pompeius's slave, 2 victories, 2 crowns.
Gaius Masonius, 7 victories, 4 crowns
Phileros, Domitius's slave, 12 victories, 11 crowns
Optatus, Salvius's slave, novice
Gaius Alfidius, novice
Murmillones: Quintus Cleppius, novice
Julius, novice
Retiarii: ...., novice

ILS 5083a = CIL 9.466: from Venusia. Although this tablet was found together with ILS 5083, the lettering on the two tablets is different, so they were probably not both parts of the same monument. This tablet also lists a gladiator *familia*, but the *lanista*'s name is missing.

Oceanus, Avilius's slave, novice
Sagittarius: Dorus, Pisius's slave, 6 victories, 4 crowns
Veles: Mycter, Ofilius's slave, 2 victories

[46] This does not mean that Terentius himself actually killed the gladiators and animals. Rather, since he was the one putting on the *munus*, he was responsible for the deaths in the arena.
[47] Crowns were apparently given to gladiators for particularly well-fought victories, perhaps those in which they killed their opponents (that is, victories without *missio*).

Hoplomachus: Phaeder, Avilius's slave, novice
Thraeces: Donatus, Nerius's slave, 12 victories, 8 crowns
Hilario, Arrius's slave, 7 victories, 5 crowns
Aquilia, Pisius's slave, 12 victories, 6 crowns
Quartio, Munilius's slave, 1 victory
Gaius Perpernius, novice
Murmillones: Amicus, Munilius's slave, 1 victory
Quintus Fabius, 5 victories, 3 crowns
Eleuther, Munilius's slave, 1 victory
Gaius Memmius, 3 victories, 2 crowns
Anteros, Munilius's slave, 2 victories
Atlans, Donius's slave, 4 victories, 1 crown
Essedarius: Inclutus, Arrius's slave, 5 victories, 2 crowns
Samnite: Strabo, Donius's slave, 3 victories, 2 crowns
Retiarius: Gaius Clodius, 2 victories
Scissor: Marus Caecilius, novice
Gallus: Quintus Granius, novice

ILS 5086 = CIL 5.4511, tombstone at Brixia

Sacred to the memory of Volsueno, freed at his eighth fight.[48] His friends the Thraeces erected this.

ILS 5087 = CIL 12.3332, tombstone at Nemausis

From this and other tombstones, we can determine that gladiators were relatively young. See additional tombstones in chapter 5, erected by the gladiators' widows.

Lucius Sestius Latinus the trainer dedicated this to Quintus Vettius Gracilis, a Thraex who won three crowns, aged 25, from Spain.

ILS 5089 = CIL 6.10197, tombstone at Rome

Sacred to the memory of Macedonus, novice Thraex, Alexandrian, well-deserving, erected by all the Thraeces together. He lived 22 years 8 months 12 days.

ILS 5099 = CIL 6.10181, at Rome

These memorials show that there were separate trainers for gladiators of different types.

Gaius Cassius Gemellus, trainer of *hoplomachi*.

ILS 5103 = CIL 6.10175, at Rome

Aulus Postumius Acoemetus, trainer of *murmillones*.

ILS 5113 = CIL 10.7297, somewhere in Sicily. To "receive *missio* standing" may mean the fight was declared a draw before either competitor was knocked

---

[48] This could also mean "a free man (an *auctoratus*) who fought eight times."

down and at the mercy of the other.

Flamma, *secutor*, lived 30 years, fought 34 times, conquered 21, received *missio* standing 9 times, received *missio* 4 times, Syrian by birth. Delicatus erected this for a deserving fellow-fighter.

ILS 5123 = CIL 5.563, at Tergeste

Constantius who gave the *munus* has given this tomb to his gladiators because the *munus* was well received. To Decoratus the *retiarius*, who killed Caeruleus and died himself; as both died by the same sword, so the same pyre covers both. Decoratus the *secutor*, after 9 fights, left his wife Valeria grieving for the first time.

ILS 5150 = CIL 10.4195. Gladiator *munera* frequently had musical accompaniment. This epigram is in verse, appropriate for a musician, though the meter is somewhat irregular.

Stay a moment, please, traveler hurrying by, and learn briefly about my death, since you anticipate such a day will come for you, too. I was called Justus, after my mother, not my father; I was born of a father who was poor but rich in reputation. I was a *tibicen*, modulating my song on the double pipe and with Mars's song rousing the gladiators to arms. I lived 21 years, 11 months, 29 days, and died a bitter death. Erected by his parents to an incomparable son.

ILS 5156 = CIL 6226, ILS 5157 = CIL 6227

Amphitheaters required support staff. These two inscriptions are in the tomb of the Statilius family, so it is plausible that Charito and Menander worked in the amphitheater constructed by a member of that family, Titus Statilius Taurus, in 29 BC.

Charito, amphitheater guard
Menander, freedman, doorman at the amphitheater

Chapter 3

Chariots and Circus *Ludi*

These selections describe chariot races, their drivers, and their fans. We are fortunate to have many monuments with inscriptions for charioteers; they give us a good idea of what a driver's career might be like and how much money he could win. Chariot races were so familiar and so popular that they turn up in all different kinds of literature, from short, light poems like Martial's to serious epics like the Ennius's *Annals* and Virgil's *Georgics*. The poems quoted here range in time through the entire literary history of Rome, from the second century BC (Ennius) to the fifth century AD (Sidonius). See also the excerpt from the *Life of Nero* in chapter 4, and ILS 5282, referring to the Purple faction, in chapter 5.

Ennius

The following selections show Ennius's use of sporting metaphors and give some idea what events may have been important in his time.

Annals 86-91

Romulus and Remus contend for the right to name the new city, Roma or Remora. It is a matter of great moment to all their men which of the two should hold sway. They wait, just as when the consul intends to give the signal, everyone eagerly watches the mouth of the starting-gate which will soon let the painted chariots come forth. Just so the people waited and held their breath.

Annals 388-389

We do not know what Ennius was comparing to the horse. It is possible that this fragment, quoted by Cicero, comes from the end of the epic, and it is Ennius himself who is old.

Just as a strong horse, who has often won at Olympia in the last lap, now rests worn out by old age, ...

Virgil, *Georgics* 1.511-514

Just as Ennius used similes from chariot racing, so did the later epic poet.

Godless Mars rages through the entire world, just as when chariots spill out from the starting gates onto the racetrack, and the charioteer,

24

clinging vainly to the reins, is swept along by the horses; the chariot does not heed the reins.

Ovid

The two selections given here, from different love poems, go together nicely; there are lots of phrases and even whole lines repeated in both. Ovid chooses the circus *ludi* rather than a gladiator *munus* for his flirtation because at gladiator shows women had to sit in the back, separate from the men. At the races, however, seating arrangements were less restrictive.

Art of Love 1.135-176

The theory.

You shouldn't avoid the contests of famous horses: the Circus is very convenient and holds a lot of people. You don't need a secret hand-signal to talk to her, or a nod of recognition from far away: there is nothing to keep you from sitting right next to your mistress. Sit as close as you can, with your side touching hers; in fact, the lines between seats[49] bring you close together even if you don't want it. It's one of the rules of the place that you can touch the girl. You can find a way to strike up a conversation starting from what everyone else is saying; ask her whose horses are coming, and be sure to back whichever team she favors. When the procession goes by, full of ivory gods and goddesses, applaud Lady Venus enthusiastically. If it happens that a bit of dust falls on the girl's lap, it must be brushed off, and by your fingers. If there's no dust, brush it off anyway. Find any excuse to make yourself useful. If her robe trails on the ground, pull it up and carefully brush the dirt off it; then, as a reward for your labors, it may happen that she lets you catch a glimpse of her legs. Also keep an eye on whoever is sitting behind you, so he doesn't push at her soft back with his hard knee. It's the little things that get her attention: it has been useful to many men to be able to brush off dust with a gentle hand, or to stir up a breeze with the program, or to put a footstool under a delicate foot. The Circus offers such opportunities to a new love; so does the gloomy sand spread in the forum. Venus's boy has often fought in that arena, and many a one who has watched other men wounded has gotten a wound of his own. While he talks, and touches her hand, and asks for a program, and asks who's winning (after he's placed a bet), he moans from his wound and feels the arrow fly: he is himself part of the *munus*. What about when Caesar brought in Persian and Cecropian ships in a simulated naval battle? Surely young men and girls came from every land, and the whole world was in the City. Who couldn't find someone to love in that crowd? How many people burned with foreign love!

---

[49] Seats in the Circus were stone benches or steps, with inscribed lines to mark off one person's place from the next.

Amores ("Love Poems") 3.2

A case-study in the application of the above theory.

"I'm not sitting here out of any love for famous horses, but I do pray that the one you're rooting for wins. I've come here so I can talk to you and sit with you, and so that you may not be unaware of the love you've inspired in me. You're watching the races, I'm watching you: let's each feast our eyes on what pleases us.

What a lucky man is the charioteer you favor. Do you happen to care about him? I wish the same thing would happen to me. Once released from the sacred starting-gate I'll stand bravely and let the horses pull; sometimes I'll give them their heads, sometimes I'll score their backs with the whip, now I'll just brush the turning-post with the inside wheel. If I catch a glimpse of you as I'm racing, I'll linger in front of you and the reins will fall out of my hands. Oh, the Pisaean spear could hardly bring down Pelops once he got a look at your face, Hippodamia! He won because of his girl's support; may we each win by ours.

Why are you trying to get away? The lines between seats bring us close together; this is one of the convenient rules of the Circus. You there, whoever you are, on the right, give the girl a break: you're hurting her. And you, behind us, pull back your legs, if you have any decency, and don't press her back with your bony knee. Your robe is trailing on the ground; pull it up, or, see, I'll take it in my hands. Unfriendly robe, that covers such nice legs: you get to see everything and you hide it from me. Atalanta ran away on legs like these, that Milanion hoped to get his hands on. Legs like these are Diana's ornament just as much as her quiver, as she hunts wild beasts and is stronger than they are. I haven't seen yours, and I yearn to; what if I did? You pour fuel on the fire and water into the sea. I suppose, from what I have seen, that everything else will please me, too, that now lies hidden under that pretty robe.

Meanwhile, would you like me to summon the gentle breeze by fanning you with my program? Or is this heat more in myself than in the air, since a woman's love burns my captive heart? While I'm talking, a bit of dust gets on your white robe: filthy dust, get away from her snowy body!

Now the procession comes: speak no ill-omened words, but cheer and applaud as the gold goes by. First comes Victory with her wings spread out: goddess, grant that my love be victorious. Applaud Neptune, you who trust so much in the waves; I want nothing to do with the sea—I'll stick to the land. Soldier, applaud your Mars; I hate war; peace is pleasanter, and in peace we discover love. May Phoebus stand by his prophets and Phoebe by her hunters, and craftsmen turn their hands to you, Minerva. Stand up as rustic Ceres and soft Bacchus come by. The fighters love Pollux, the riders Castor. I applaud you, gentle Venus, and your boys with powerful bows. Goddess, look with favor on my undertaking and give sense to my new mistress, that she may permit herself to be loved. The goddess nods and gives a sign of approval. Now I ask that you promise me what the goddess has promised: you will be more of a goddess to me than Venus herself. I swear by you and by all the gods in the procession that you will be my mistress for all time.

But your legs are dangling. If it would help, you can push your toes through the railing.

Now the track is empty and the praetor is putting the chariots into the starting-gate for the main spectacle. I see who you're rooting for. May the one you favor win. The horses themselves seem to know you're behind them. Oh dear, he makes a wide turn at the turning-post. What are you doing? The next one is getting past on the inside. What are you doing, you fool? You're going to lose the girl's good wishes; I want you to get good hold of the left-side reins. We're backing a coward. Call them back, Roman citizens, shake your togas on all sides and say you want to start over. Look, they are calling them back. So all these togas being shaken out don't mess up your hair, you may tuck your head down on my breast. They've opened up the starting gates again, and the contestants of each color fly out. Now win this time! Get into that open space! May my wish and my lady's wish be granted.

My lady's wish is granted; my wishes remain. He's got his victory palm, mine is still to be sought."

She laughs and her expressive eyes promise something: "That's enough of that. Give me the rest someplace else."

Inscriptions

Inscriptions relating to charioteers include gravestones, other memorials, and some graffiti.

ILS 5283 = CIL 6.10051, at Rome. The years are consecutive from AD 13 through AD 25.

Carisia Nesis Scirtis, freedman, driver for the White faction.[50]

In the consulate of Lucius Munatius and Gaius Silius, *quadriga*,[51] won 1, 2nd 1, 3rd 1

In the consulate of Sextus Pompeius and Sextus Appuleius, won 1, 2nd 1, 3rd 2

In the consulate of Drusus Caesar and Gaius Norbanus, won 1, 2nd 2, 3rd 5

In the consulate of Sisenna Statilius and Lucius Scribonius, won 2, recalled[52] 1, 2nd 5, 3rd 5

---

[50] See the glossary for more information on the factions or "colors."

[51] A *quadriga* is a four-horse chariot; a *biga* has two horses.

[52] Sometimes the chariots would be called back to the starting line and the race would be started over; this may have been in response to mistakes in religious rituals, or to fouls in the race. Compare the selection from Ovid's *Amores*, above, in which the racers are called back.

In the consulate of Gaius Caelius and Lucius Pomponius, won 2, recalled 1, 2nd 8, 3rd 6

In the 3rd consulate of Titus Caesar and the 2nd of Germanicus Caesar, 2nd 7, 3rd 12

In the consulate of Marcus Silanus and Lucius Norbanus, recalled 1, 2nd 5, 3rd 5

In the consulate of Marcus Valerius and Marcus Aurelius, 2nd 3, 3rd 4

In the 4th consulate of Titus Caesar and the 2nd of Drusus Caesar, 2nd 2, 3rd 5

In the consulate of Decimus Haterius Agrippa and Sulpicius, 2nd 3, 3rd 4

In the consulate of Gaius Asinius and Gaius Antistius Vetus, recalled 1, 2nd 1, 3rd 5

In the consulate of Servius Cornelius Cethegus and Lucius Visellius, 2nd 1, 3rd 4

In the consulate of Cossus Cornelius Lentulus and Marcus Asinius, 3rd 2

Grand total: in the *quadriga* 7 victories, recalled 4 times, second 39, third 60; also *iustiale*[53] 1 and 6-horse chariot twice.

ILS 5278 = CIL 6.33950, at Rome, AD 35

Fuscus, driver for the Greens, age 24, won 53 times at Rome, twice in the *ludi* for the goddess Dia, once in the *ludus* given by Bovillis, won one palm, called back twice and won. He was the first of all the drivers to win on the day he was sent out. Machao erected this to preserve his memory in the consulate of Gaius Cestius and Marcus Servilius.

ILS 5284 = CIL 6.10055, at Rome, around AD 68. The name of the driver is missing from this gravestone, but the record appears to be complete.

.... driver for the Blue faction, died in the consulate of Appius Annius Gallus and Lucius Verulanus Severus, on 23 August. Won with the *quadriga* 47 times, second 131, third 146. With *biga* won 9, second 8, third 8. With *adgens quadriga*[54] won twice, recalled twice; in instaurations came third once. Received honors[55] 354 times. Lived 25 years. Crispina Meroe erected this.

ILS 5301 = CIL 2.4313, at Tarragona, Spain. This epigram is in verse, except for the last line, which is in Greek. It quotes lines from Virgil's *Aeneid*, so must be later than that poem (which was written at the beginning of the first century AD), but it does not include a date.

---

[53] Unclear; this may refer to a race in which there was no winner.

[54] What an *adgens quadriga* was is not known.

[55] This means finishing first, second, or third—in other words, not last.

To Fuscus of the Blue faction we have consecrated this altar at our own expense. We loved him greatly and are eager and determined that everyone may know this monument and pledge of our love. Your fame is complete; you have deserved praise for your racing. You competed with many and though a poor man you feared nothing; though you had enemies you were always strong and silent; you lived beautifully, and now you have met a mortal's fate.

Passer-by, whoever you are, search for such a man as this. Stand and read, if you remember, if you know who this man was. Everyone may fear fortune, but you will say this one thing: Fuscus has an inscription and a tomb. The stone covers his bones; he is well. Fortune, you will be strong. We have poured gentle tears and now pour wine. We pray you may lie quietly. There is no one like you.

Your competition will always be remembered.

Juvenal, *Satire* 7.112-114

Some satirical perspective on the prize-money statistics in the gladiators' inscriptions.

If you really want to rake it in, look at Lacerta of the Reds: he's made as much as 100 lawyers leave to their sons.

Martial, *Epigrams*

10.9, comparing the fame of a poet and a circus horse. See ILS 5289 below for another reference to this horse.

With eleven feet and syllables[56] at a time, and much wit, though not too impudent, Martial is known to the nations and to the people. Why do you envy me? I'm no more famous than Andraemo the horse.

10.48, a proposed dinner party. The appropriate small-talk for an informal occasion was "of the Greens and the Blues," that is, about the races.

The tumult of the close of the temple announces the eighth hour to Io, the Pharian heifer, and a troop armed with the javelin goes back and forth. This hour tempers the warm baths, an early hour breathes out too much steam, and the sixth hour warms unrestrained Nero.

Stella, Nepos, Canius, Cerialis, Flaccus, are you coming? The couch holds seven, we are six, add Lupus.

The housekeeper brought me mallows to soothe the stomach; we'll have the varied wealth of the garden, including lettuce and cut leeks, but not mint that makes you belch or grass that makes you lustful. Slices of

---

[56] This is a reference to the metrical form of the poem: the eleven-syllable line called the "Phalacean hendecasyllable."

egg will crown rue-flavored fish, and sow's udder will be poached with tuna from the sea. These will be the appetizers; dinner will be just one course, a kid taken from the jaws of a cruel wolf, with dainty bits cut up before serving, and fava beans; a chicken and a ham will be added to make three main dishes. I'll put out sweet apples when we're sated, and I'll serve a big jug of Nomentine wine with no sediment, from Frontinus's consulate.

There will be jokes and laughing without bitterness; no one needs to fear the party will break up too early, and we won't talk of any unpleasant subjects: let my guests talk of the Greens and the Blues, and may our cups not turn anyone into a defendant.

Inscription

ILS 5289 = CIL 6.10052. This Andraemo is probably the same horse referred to in Martial 10.9 above.

Scorpus won with these horses: Pegasus, Elates, Andraemo, Cotynus.

Petronius, *Satyricon* sec. 70

After dinner, slaves are invited in for the leftovers. Philargyrus, Carrio, and Menophila are Trimalchio's slaves, and it appears Menophila had the same name as a driver for the Green faction.

Now Fortunata wanted to start dancing, Scintilla was applauding more than she was talking, and Trimalchio said, "Philargyrus and Carrio may come to the table. And, if you're the well-known Green fan, tell your messmate Menophila he can come too." What more? We were practically pushed off the couches as the slaves took over the whole dining room. I recognized above me the cook who'd made goose out of pork, stinking of brine and spices. And he wasn't satisfied just to recline but started right in imitating the tragedy of Ephesus, occasionally trying to get his master to bet on whether the Greens would get first place at the next Circus.

Cassius Dio, *Roman History* 67.4

This passage is our main source for Domitian's "expansion teams." It shows Domitian trying to leave his mark on history.

Domitian changed the name of October, the month when he was born, to "Domitianus." He established two additional types of chariot-drivers, the gold and the purple. He gave many tokens for gifts to the spectators.

Inscriptions

ILS 5285 = CIL 6.10050, at Rome. The year of his first victory is AD 115. The celebration of Claudius's anniversary in the consulate of Glabrio is AD 124, so

Crescens's career lasted at least 9 years. That is, he must have started racing at age 13 or even younger.

Crescens, driver for the Blue faction, Mauritanian by birth, 22 years old. First won with the *quadriga* in the consulate of Lucius Vipsanius and Messalla. On Nerva's birthday came 24th with these horses: Circius, Acceptor, Delicatus, Cotynus. When Glabrio replaced Messalla as consul, on the birthday of the divine Claudius, he started in 686 races and won 47. Among those, in races for single *quadriga* he won 19, in races for pairs 23, and in races for 3 he won 5. He won after being passed[57] once, led through the whole race 8 times, won at the finish line 38 times. He took second place 130 times, third 111. He received prizes of 1,558,346 sesterces.

ILS 5287 = CIL 6.10048, at Rome, AD 146. The extensive career of Diocles spanned 24 years, starting when he was 18, and three of the four factions. His 4,257 races included: 1,462 victories, 861 second place, 576 third, 1 fourth, and 1,351 out of the money in chariots with four or more horses, and 6 victories in two-horse chariots. He raced in many different events: races for one, two, or three chariots of each color (making 4, 8, or 12 on the track at once), races in which colors paired off (usually Green and Red against Blue and White), races for very large purses, races with large numbers of horses. Diocles's name indicates that he was probably a freedman. There are gaps in the text because parts of the stone are missing.

Gaius Appuleius Diocles, driver for the Red faction, Lusitanian by birth, aged 42 years 7 months 23 days. He first drove for the White faction in the consulate of Acilius Aviola and Corellius Pansa [AD 122]. He first won in the same faction in the consulate of Manlius Acilius Glabrio and Gaius Bellicius Torquatus [AD 124]. He first drove for the Green faction in the consulate of Torquatus Asprenatis for the second time and Annius Libo [AD 128]. He first won in the Red faction in the consulate of Laenatis Pontianus and Antonius Rufino [AD 131].

Total: drove a *quadriga* for 24 years, sent from the gate 4,257 times, won 1,462, from the *pompa*[58] 110. In races for single *quadriga* he won 1,064, taking the largest prizes 92 times: the 30,000-sesterces prize 32 times, 3 of these in a 6-horse chariot; the 40,000-sesterces prize 28 times, twice in a 6-horse chariot; the 50,000-sesterces prize 28 times, once in a 6-horse chariot; the 60,000-sesterces prize 3 times. In races for pairs of chariots he won 347 times, and with a three-horse chariot won 15,000 sesterces 4 times. In races for three chariots he won 51 times. He received honors 1,000 times.

---

[57] The categories "won after being passed," "led the whole race," and "won at the finish line," along with "came from behind" which does not appear here, seem to have been technical terms; see also ILS 5287, the career of Diocles.

[58] Winning "from the *pompa*" means winning the first race of the day, the one immediately after the opening procession (*pompa*). It is not clear why this was a separate category; perhaps it was harder to win the first race because the procession made the horses nervous.

He took second place 861 times, third 576, fourth with a 1,000-sesterces prize once, and finished out of the money 1,351 times. He won jointly with a Blue driver 10 times, with a White 91, and shared the 20,000-sesterces prize twice. His total winnings were 35,863,120 sesterces. In addition in a *biga* he won 1,000 sesterces three times alone, jointly with a White driver once, and jointly with a Green driver twice.

He won leading from the start 815 times, coming from behind 67, after being passed 36, in various ways 42, and at the finishing line 502. He won against Greens 216 times, against Blues 205, and against Whites 81.[59] Nine horses had 100 victories with him and one had 200.

His distinctions:

... in the year when he first won twice with a *quadriga*, he won at the finishing line twice. It said in the daily gazette that Avilius Teres had been the first in his faction to win 1,011, and he won most often in one year in races for single chariot, but Diocles that same year first won over 100 victories, winning 103, 83 of them in races for single chariot. Then, increasing his glory, he went ahead of Thallus of his faction, who was the first in the Red faction to.... But Diocles was the most distinguished of all drivers, since in one year he won 134 with another driver's lead horse, 118 in races for single chariot, which put him ahead of all the drivers who ever competed in circus *ludi*.

It is noted by all, with well-deserved admiration, that in one year with unfamiliar lead horses, with Cotynus and Pompeianus as the inside pair, he won 99 times, getting the 60,000-sesterces prize once, 50,000 sesterces 4 times, 40,000 sesterces once, and 30,000 twice.

... of the Green faction, winner 1,025 times, and Flavius Scorpus, winner 2,048 times, and Pompeius Musclosus, winner 3,550 times. Those three drivers won 6,632 times and won the 50,000-sesterces prize 28 times, but Diocles, the most distinguished driver of all, with 1,462 victories, won the 50,000-sesterces prize 29 times.

Diocles has the most noble glory, since Fortunatus of the Green faction, who won with Tusco the champion 386 times, won the 50,000-sesterces prize 9 times, but Diocles with the champion Pompeianus won 152 times, and won the 50,000-sesterces prize 10 times and the 60,000-sesterces prize once.

Diocles was particularly strong in new events. In one day he raced twice with 6-horse chariots for a 40,000-sesterces prize and was victorious both times.... a chariot with seven horses harnessed together, a number of horses never before seen, in a contest for 50,000 sesterces, he won with Abigeius and without using the whip. In other contests for 30,000 sesterces....

Among drivers with 1,000 or more victories, Pontius Epaphroditus

---

[59] Since 216 + 205 + 81 = 502, these three numbers may refer only to the close victories at the finishing line.

of the Blue faction seems to have the first place, who in the time of our emperor Antoninus Augustus Pius was sole victor 1,467 times, 909 in races for single chariot, but Diocles got ahead of him, winning 1,462 times, 1,064 in races for single chariot. In his day Pontius Epaphroditus won 467 races at the finish line, but Diocles won 502.

In the year when he won 127 times, Diocles won 103 with Abigeius, Lucidus, and Pompeianus.

Among distinguished drivers many have won with African horses: Pontius Epaphroditus of the Blue faction won 134 with Bubalus, Pompeius Musclosos of the Green faction won 115 with .... Diocles has outdone them, winning 152 with Pompeianus, 144 in races for single chariot. More gloriously, with Cotynus, Galata, Abigeius, Lucidus, and Pompeius he won 445 times, 397 in races for single chariot.

ILS 5286 = CIL 6.10049, near Rome, two statues, each with its own inscription, and a poem in Greek below them. No date is specified.

1. Marcus Aurelius Polynices, native of Rome, who lived 29 years 9 months 5 days, won the palm 739 times as follows: as a Red 655, as a Green 55, as a Blue 12, as a White 17. Won the 40,000-sesterces prize 3 times, the 30,000-sesterces prize 26 times, the "pure"[60] prize 11 times. With 8-horse chariot 8 times, with 10-horse chariot 9, with 6-horse chariot 3.

2. Marcus Aurelius Mollicius Tatianus, native of Rome, who lived 20 years 8 months 7 days, who won 125 victory palms as follows: as a Red 89, as a Green 24, as a Blue 5, as a White 7; won the 40,000-sesterces prize twice.

3. The famous charioteer Polynices brought up two sons in his fatherland Rome, Macaris and Tatianus. They shared his fate in the stadium. The two brave sons met their end together.[61]

ILS 5298 = CIL 6.10057, at Rome, undated

Sacred to the memory of Aurelius Heraclides, driver for the Blue faction and trainer of the above-mentioned faction and the Green. Marcus Ulpius Apolaustianus erected this for a well-deserving colleague.

ILS 5313 = CIL 6.10046, at Rome. The date is unknown. This inscription shows how many supporting jobs there were in a chariot-racing *familia*.

The *quadriga familia* of Titus Ateius Capito of the Red faction,[62] Chrestus as treasurer, gave jars of oil to the *decuriones*,[63] as listed below: Marcus Vipsanius Migionis; Docimus, overseer; Chrestus, *conditor*; Epaphrae,

---

[60] It is not known what the "pure" prize was, perhaps a purse of 15,000 sesterces.

[61] Although chariot racing was not a blood sport like gladiator fighting, it could be quite dangerous; accidents could happen just as in modern horse races or harness races.

[62] This phrase is a bit obscure; it has also been taken to mean "of the Purple faction" or the name of a co-owner of the *familia*.

[63] These *decuriones* are leaders of the *familia*, not of the municipal government.

steward; Menander, driver; Apollonius, driver; Cerdonis, driver; Liccaeus, driver; Helletis, assistant to the *conditor*; Publius Quinctius Primus; Hyllus, doctor; Anterotis, *tentor*; Antiochus, blacksmith; Parnacis, *tentor*; Marcus Vipsanius Calamus; Marcus Vipsanius Dareus; Eros, *tentor*; Marcus Vipsanius Faustus; Hilarus, driver; Nicander, driver; Epigonus, driver; Alexander, driver; Nicephorus, *spartor*; Alexionis, *morator*; ..., messenger.

ILS 5288 = CIL 6.10047, originally on the Via Flaminia. There are three separate inscriptions on this monument. Since there is a reference to "victories listed above," we know there were originally more, but the stone is lost and all we have is a copy made in about the ninth century AD. The original text may be as late as the fourth century or as early as the second. Gutta is one of the very few drivers we know of to win a race including sixteen chariots, four from each color.

1. Publius Aelius Gutta Calpurnianus, son of Marius Rogatus. I won with these horses for the Blue faction: Germinator, black from Africa, 92. Silvanus, red from Africa, 105. Nitidus, gold from Africa, 52. Saxo, black from Africa, 60. And I won major prizes: 50,000 sesterces once, 40,000 sesterces 9 times, 30,000 sesterces 17 times.

2. Publius Aelius Gutta Calpurnianus, son of Marius Rogatus. I won 1,000 palms for the Green faction with these horses: Danaus, bay from Africa, 19. Ocianus, black, 209. Victor, red, 429. Vindex, bay, 157. And I won major prizes: 40,000 sesterces 3 times, 30,000 sesterces 3 times.

3. I won 1,127 palms as described above:

In the White faction 102, called back 2, 30,000 sesterces 1, 40,000 sesterces 1, from the *pompa* 4, with novice horses 1, in races for single chariot[64] 83, in races for pairs of chariots 17, in races for three chariots 2.

In the Red faction I won 78, called back 1, 30,000 sesterces 1, in races for single chariot 42, in races for pairs of chariots 32, in races for three chariots 3, in races for four chariots 1.

In the Blue faction I won 583, 30,000 sesterces 17, once with six horses, 40,000 sesterces 9, 50,000 sesterces 1, from the *pompa* 35, with three-horse chariot won 10,000 sesterces 1 and 25,000 sesterces 1, with novice horses 1, at the quinquennial sacred games 1, called back 1. In races for single chariot 334, in races for pairs of chariots 184, in races for three chariots 65.

In the Green faction I won 364, 30,000 sesterces 1, 40,000 sesterces 2, the chariot-and-foot race[65] for 60,000 sesterces 1, from the *pompa* 6, in races for single chariot 116, in races for pairs of chariots 184, in races

---

[64] "Single chariot" means one chariot from each of the four factions. Races for pairs would involve two from each color, working together against the other colors; similarly, there were races for three or four chariots from each color (making 12 or 16 chariots on the track in total).
[65] The "chariot-and-foot" race probably involved runners jumping down from the chariot at a certain point and finishing the race on foot. There were similar events in some of the Greek festivals.

for three chariots 64.

I built this monument for myself while still alive.

Apollinaris Sidonius, 23.307-427

Sidonius wrote the poem this extract is taken from for his friend Consentius of Narbonne, probably between AD 460 and 465. Although the race described here involves amateurs (Consentius was a poet, not a charioteer), it seems to be run under the same rules the professional drivers used. Colors are assigned by lot. Sidonius does not tell us which color Consentius has, but he implies that Blue and White are teamed up against Green and Red in the usual way. This is a race for four chariots in two pairs, so Consentius's eventual victory is shared with a partner of another color. As the chariots go counter-clockwise, the left is the inside lane, closest to the turning-post, and the right is the outside, nearer the spectators.

As the sun had completed another circuit, Janus was opening the doors of the new year and bringing back the chariots. It is Caesar's custom to adorn this day with twin *ludi, ludi* always called private. Then noble youths make a grim replica of the Olympics and the plain of Elis with the thronging of their chariots. Now the urn calls you out and a strident acclamation rises hoarsely from the crowd. Then, where the door is and the consuls' seats, and the wall that goes around the six starting-gates and forms arches to enclose them, there are four chariots. You get in to the chariot assigned you by lot and take its curved reins. So does your colleague and at the same time so do the opponents. The colors flash: blue and white, green and red, the signs under which you race. An assistant's hands hold the bits and the bridles, braid the manes out of sight into tidy knots, and meanwhile they encourage the horses with cajoling pats, teaching them delightful eagerness. The horses whinny at the closed gate and lean against the bolts, breathing out through the gates until the course, not yet filled with horses, is filled with their breath. They push, jostle, pull, push back, grow excited, jump. They are both fearful and fearsome. With unrestrained, nervous feet they strike the walls.

At last the trumpeter calls forth the waiting chariots with a shrill sound from his horn, and pours them out into the field of play. No three-pronged thunderbolt, no arrow propelled by Scythian sinew, no swift shooting star, no leaden storm from Balearic slingshots ever shattered the serenity of the sky as they do. The earth yields to the wheels; the air is besmirched by their dusty motion.

They press their horses on, controlling them with blows. Stretching far forward from their cars, leaning their breasts over their coursers, they smite the riderless backs. You could not quickly determine whether the pole or the wheels supported the drivers.

Now as you finish off the open space, the track, artfully constricted, closes you up, where the moat has stretched out a long, low, two-fold wall. As the far turning-post sends you all back, your colleague gets in front of the two who are passing you; you were thus fourth in the revolving rotation. Those in the middle aimed to harry the leader from the right, and if he in response would open up the left side, bringing his reins to the podium, there would be space for a chariot to slip inside.

You, attempting the same feat, keep close hold on your horses and with all your skill hold back for the seventh lap. The others encourage their teams with voice and hands, and sweat from the drivers and the wing-footed steeds drips everywhere on the track. Noise strikes the fans to their hearts while the drivers and horses alike feel the heat of the race and the cold of fear.

Thus the first lap, thus the second, so too the third and fourth. But on the fifth circuit, the leader can no longer bear the pressure of his pursuers, so he turns back, recognizing the speed he'd called for had exhausted his team. Now on the sixth lap, as the crowd clamors for prizes, the opposing side feared no force of yours, and went coolly along on the familiar track. Suddenly you put new tension on the bits and the yokes and lean on your front foot. Just as Pelops made Pisa tremble behind his chariot as he carried off Hippodameia, so you drive on your team.

As one opponent aims for a tight, short course around the turning-post, you provoke him, and he cannot bend his team's course: they are carried straight on by their speed. He's passed you, out of control, but you have artfully passed him by holding back.

The other, gloating in the applause, goes too far to the right, next to the seats. As he tries to turn back to the course, goading his steeds with the whip, but too late, you go past him on the straightaway.

Now the enemy, pursuing you recklessly and hoping his colleague is already first, comes boldly across the course to ram your wheel. His horses crumple. The shameless mob of their legs goes into the wheels and breaks the spokes one after another, until the center of the wheel is full of cracking sounds and the rim stops the flying feet. He himself falls fifth from the collapsing chariot, making a massive mountain of ruin, and staining his fallen face with blood.

The whole catastrophe is accompanied by crashing noise, such as cypress-bearing Lycaeus has never heard, nor has shady Ossa raised such noise when buffeted by swift hurricanes, nor do the waves of Sicily or the briny whirlpool that defends the Bosphorus crash thus when roiled by the south wind.

Then the fair emperor orders silk to be added to the victory palms and coronets to the torques, reward for achievement; for the shamed losers, multicolored shaggy woolen rugs.

Chapter 4

Theater, Greek Athletics, and Other Events

The following passages describe spectacles and competitions other than gladiator combats and chariot races. These include novelty fights, *venationes*, staged battles, mythical re-enactments, other executions, and theater. They also include Greek athletic contests: boxing, wrestling, or foot races. Several of these selections describe complete festivals, giving an idea of what went together. Note, particularly in the description of Augustus's *ludi saeculares* ("century games"), that there are always sacrifices and prayers to the gods.

The great Greek athletic festivals (the Olympic, Pythian, Isthmian, and Nemean games) were still held after Greece came under Roman rule. Originally only free Greek citizens, men and boys, competed, but under the Roman Empire some Romans were also allowed to participate. The events in a Greek competition included boxing, wrestling, sprints (roughly 200 meters), longer foot races, and chariot racing. Some Greek festivals also included competitions for singers, musicians, or actors.

See also Livy 39.22 in chapter I about the first exhibition of Greek-style athletics at Rome, and Cicero, *Letters to Friends* 7.1 in ch. 7, on theatrical *ludi*.

Theater

Theater in Rome included tragedy, comedy, mime, and pantomime. Tragedies and comedies were often adapted from Greek plays, and were performed by actors wearing masks. Mimes were musicals, and the performers did not necessarily wear masks. In pantomimes, the main actor would dance but would not speak or sing, and he would usually play all the roles himself.

Terence, *Hecyra* 1-57

Hecyra ("The Mother-in-Law") was performed three times. After the disastrous first performance, at the *ludi Megalenses* in 165 BC, a short prologue was added explaining why the performance was to be an "old" play rather than a new one. After the equally disastrous second performance, as part of *ludi* for a funeral in 160, a longer prologue was added, explaining again and asking for the audience's co-operation. The third performance was successful, as far as we know; it took place at the *ludi Romani* later in 160 BC. The speaker of the second prologue is an older friend of Terence's, old enough to have worked with Caecilius, a playwright about a generation older.

Prologue 1

Hecyra is the name of this play. When it was put on as a new play, a disastrous new flaw[66] came up, so the play couldn't be watched and no one got to know it: the audience was stupefied with amazement watching a rope-dancer. Now here it is again as a new play. Its author hadn't wanted to re-perform it the first time, so he could re-sell it this time. You know his other plays: now get to know this one.

Prologue 2

Though I look like a prologue-speaker, I'm really here to plead a case. Permit me to prevail and to enjoy the same rights now that I'm old as I did when I was a little younger. I used to tidy up new plays so they'd become old ones and not die with their authors. When Caecilius would give me his new ones, I got booed off the stage with some of them, and barely held on with others. Because I always knew the luck of the stage is a chancy thing, I supported his indefinite hope with my definite work, and performed the same plays again, so I'd get more new ones from him. I didn't want to drive him out of the business. I got people to watch his plays, and then they liked them. That's how I brought Caecilius back to his rightful place, when his enemies had unfairly almost driven him away from the work he loved—the theater. If I'd thought his writing wasn't any good, and if I'd set my mind to scaring him off, getting him out of this business, I could easily have kept him from writing any more plays.

So, listen patiently to the case I'm pleading now. I'm reviving the *Hecyra*, which I have never yet been able to put on in peace and quiet—such disastrous things have happened to it. But your perceptive understanding, added to our hard work, will forestall another disaster. The first time I put it on, people were cheering for the boxers (and waiting for the rope-dancer), and there was such a crowd with so much shouting and screaming that I was driven out before we were done. I followed my own old rule for a new play and put it on again. This time, I was doing well with the first act, when a rumor came up that there would be gladiators, and a crowd came flying in. They made a lot of noise in shouting and fighting for seats; meanwhile I couldn't keep my place.

---

[66] If any flaw was discovered in the performance of any Roman ritual, it was necessary to do it over until the participants got it right. The re-performance was called "instauration." Because plays were part of religious festivals, they were subject to the rule of instauration just like sacrifices or public prayers. Occasionally an audience who particularly liked a play would claim there had been a flaw in its production, so it would be put on again—but that is not what happened to the *Hecyra*.

Now, today, there's no mob: there's peace and quiet. I have the opportunity to put on this play, and you can be a fitting ornament to the *ludi scaenici*. Don't let it be your fault that theater becomes just a few people's entertainment: help me out, add your influence to mine. If I've never greedily put a price on my skills, if I've always felt in my heart that the most profitable thing was to pay the most attention to your desires, let me have what I'm asking for, so that this poet, who has trusted his work to my safekeeping and himself to your good faith, will not be unfairly attacked and laughed at. Take up my cause for my sake, and give us quiet. Then other poets will want to write, and it will be profitable for me to put on new plays that I've bought at my own expense.

Horace, *Epistles* 2.1.177-200

Horace here describes the difficulties of producing plays when the audience would rather see a different kind of drama. The selection comes from a verse letter addressed to the emperor Augustus.

When Fame brings a poet to the stage in her windy chariot, the apathetic spectator deflates him and the attentive one puffs him up: such a trivial little thing it is that cuts down or builds up a heart greedy for praise. I say, "good-bye to show business," if losing makes me feel so small and winning, so big. It's enough to scare even a bold poet out of the theater. The ignorant, stupid crowd—lots of people, few of them worthy to be called "men"—ready to fight it out if some knight disagrees with them, demands a bear or a boxing-match right in the middle of the play, because that's what the little plebeians like. In fact, even the knights' pleasure has moved: it's no longer in what they hear but in deceptive visual effects. The curtain stays down[67] for four hours or longer while cavalry squadrons and infantry troops flee; then kings, once Fortune's favorites, are brought in with their hands tied. War-chariots, wagons, triumphal coaches, ships crowd in, carrying captured ivory and captured Corinthian bronze.[68] If Democritus[69] were here, he would laugh, whether it was a panther crossed with a camel[70] or a white elephant that caught the people's eyes. He'd watch the audience more than the actual plays, because it's a much better spectacle; as for the writers, he'd think they were telling a story to a deaf donkey.[71]

---

[67] In the Roman theater, the stage curtain rose up from the ground, so it was *lowered* to make the stage visible and raised at the end of a play.

[68] This is a reference to booty captured in the sack of Corinth by Romans in 146 BC.

[69] Democritus was a Greek philosopher of the fifth century BC; he is best known now for his atomic theory of matter, but Horace would have known him as the "laughing philosopher" who believed in a cheerful approach to life.

[70] A "panther crossed with a camel," or "camelopard," is a giraffe.

[71] Proverbial.

Inscriptions

ILS 5186, at Puteoli. The name of Commodus, a "bad" emperor, was erased from the monument after he died.

To Lucius Aurelius Pylades,[72] freedman of Augustus, the leading pantomimist of his day, crowned victor in sacred games four times, patron of the Parasites of Apollo,[73] priest of the synod of Artists of Dionysus, at Puteoli given the honors of a decurion and a *duovir* by decree of the decuriones, augur. Because of his love for his country and his exceptional generosity in putting on *munera* and *venationes* for all, by the kind permission of the most holy Emperor Commodus Pius Felix Augustus, the centuria Cornelia erects this monument.

ILS 5184 = CIL 6.10114, at Rome. The date of the monument is unknown; the title "Augustus" was given to all the emperors, not just the one we know by that name.

Marcus Ulpius Apolaustus, freedman of Augustus, top-rank pantomime actor, crowned 12 times in competition with actors and with all the artists of the theater.

ILS 5228 = CIL 3.3980, at Siscia

Here lies Leburna, teacher of mimes, who lived 100 years, more or less. I died several times, but never like this. I wish those who still live may live well.

Greek Athletics and Musical Contests

See also Pliny's letters 10.39 and 10.40 in chapter 6, about a theater and gymnasium in Nicea, and the selection from Propertius in chapter 5.

Suetonius, *Life of Nero*, sec. 11-12

Nero lived from 37 to 68, and became emperor after the death of Claudius in 54. He was a contemporary of Seneca, who was his teacher, and of Petronius, who was probably the "arbiter of elegance" at the imperial court. The Neronian Games are also described in the selection from Tacitus in chapter 6.

Nero gave many spectacles of various kinds: *ludi* for young men, circus spectacles, theatrical *ludi*, gladiatorial *munera*. At the young men's *ludi* he welcomed elderly ex-consuls and old married women alike as spectators. In the circus spectacles he allotted a separate place to the knights, apart from the others, and he put on chariot races with teams of four camels. At the *ludi* he gave when he assumed power (which, because his empire would be eternal, he wanted to call the *"Ludi Maximi,"* "Greatest *Ludi*"),

---

[72] "Pylades" was a cognomen or title given to outstanding pantomime actors, in honor of the actor who instituted the tragic pantomime during the reign of Augustus.

[73] The "Parasites of Apollo" was an actors' association.

many people of both sexes from the senatorial and equestrian orders had a part in the spectacle: a very well known Roman knight rode an elephant who walked the tight-rope. When Afranius's play *Fire* was produced, he permitted the actors to divide the furniture from the burning house and keep it for themselves. On each day of this spectacle he scattered all kinds of things to the people from the *missilia*: on any given day there were a thousand birds of all types, many different kinds of food, tokens for the grain distribution, clothes, gold, silver, gemstones, pearls, paintings, slaves, farm animals, even trained wild animals, and finally ships and apartment buildings and farms. He watched these *ludi* from the roof of the stage.

[Sec. 12] He put on *munera* in a wooden amphitheater near the Campus Martius which was built within a year. At his *munera* he did not kill anyone, not even the worst criminals. He had 400 senators and 600 Roman knights fight with swords, and he exhibited certain senators and knights, some of them with great fortunes and great reputations, fighting against wild beasts and ministering to the needs of the arena. He put on a naval battle with sea-animals swimming in the water. He put on the pyrrhic dance with some young men from Greece and when it was over offered each of them the privilege of Roman citizenship. One of the subjects of the pyrrhic dance was the bull who went to Pasiphae, concealed in a wooden model of a heifer, and many of those watching believed it was real. Icarus, on the first try, fell next to Nero's seat and splattered him with blood. Nero very rarely presided from the main area but usually reclined in the balcony behind a screen with holes he could see through, though later he removed it and watched from an open box.

He instituted the first quadrennial contest in all Rome in the Greek style and in three parts (musical, gymnastic, and equestrian), and called it the Neronian Games. He dedicated baths and a gymnasium and provided oil for every senator and knight. He chose magistrates for the whole contest by lot from the ex-consuls; they sat in the praetors' seats. Nero came down into the orchestra among the senators and by their consent himself received the crown for Latin oratory and singing, although everyone of good family had competed. When he was also awarded the crown for the cithara, he ordered that it be taken to the statue of Augustus. At the gymnastic contest, which went on in the Saepta, he put the first cuttings from his beard among the preparations for the ox sacrifice; they were enclosed in a gold box adorned with precious pearls, and he dedicated it at the Capitol. He invited the Vestal Virgins to the athletic spectacle because at Olympia the priestess of Demeter is permitted to watch.[74]

---

[74] Women were not allowed to attend the Olympic Games in Greece; the priestess of Demeter was the only exception. Women could attend other Greek festivals.

Life of Nero, sec. 22-24

Several emperors were amateur charioteers or gladiators. Since most charioteers and gladiators were slaves, it was something of a scandal for the emperor to take up such an activity. Nero did not compete in the Roman circus, however, but in the Greek festivals, where slaves were not allowed to compete.

Nero was passionately excited about the horses practically from the time he was born. When he was a boy the circus was all he talked about, even though he was not allowed to. If he was complaining among his classmates about how one of the Green drivers got dragged, and the *paedagogus* scolded him, he'd lie and say he was talking about Hector.[75] At the beginning of his reign, he used to play every day with an ebony chariot and a game board. He would go to even the smallest circuses by himself, first in secret, then openly, and no one ever doubted that he would show up. He did not hide the fact that he wanted to increase the number of prizes, so he prolonged the spectacles into the evening with additional races, so that faction leaders no longer thought it worth while to bring out the team except for a full day of racing. Soon he himself wanted to drive, and even more to be seen driving. He took his first training in the gardens among the slaves and the lowest class of people, then offered himself to everyone's eyes in the Circus Maximus, with some freedman dropping the *mappa* from where the magistrates usually sat.

Not content to have given this experience of his artistry at Rome, he went to Greece, as I said [in sec. 19]. The Greeks had instituted the custom of giving him all the crowns for cithara-singing when they held musical competitions. He received the crowns so gratefully that he not only gave early audiences to the legates who brought them to Rome, but even invited them to a friendly banquet. When one of them asked him to sing at dinner, he welcomed the idea and said "Only the Greeks know how to listen, and only they are worthy of me and of what I care for." He did not delay his departure for Greece, and as soon as he got to the town of Cassiope he went at once to the altar of Jupiter at Casium, where he had a favorable omen for singing. After this, he entered all the contests. Since he was only to be there for one year, he ordered that they be held in that year, even if it meant moving them from their usual times. At Olympia, against all custom, he instituted a musical contest.[76]

[Sec. 24] He also drove a chariot in many contests. At Olympia he even drove a team of 10 horses, although in one of his songs he blamed king

---

[75] Hector is the great hero of the Trojan side in the *Iliad*. When Achilles finally kills him, he drags his body behind his chariot around the walls of Troy.

[76] Although the Pythian games and other Greek festivals included competitions for singers and athletes, the Olympic games did not. Since the Olympic festival was the most prestigious, however, Nero wanted an Olympian victory.

Mithridates for exactly this. He was shaken out of the chariot, got back in, but could not hold on, so he stopped before the end of the race, but was crowned anyway. When he left the province of Greece, he granted it liberty along with the rights of Roman citizenship and a large sum of money. He announced these benefactions from the middle of the Isthmian stadium in his own voice.

Pliny the Younger, Letters 10.118, 10.119

Book 10 of Pliny's collected letters contains his correspondence with the emperor Trajan while Pliny was an imperial legate in the province of Bithynia, in northwest Asia Minor near the Black Sea.

Gaius Plinius to the emperor Trajan

My lord, the athletes whom you have rewarded for *eiselastic* contests[77] think they ought to have their rewards starting from the day on which they were crowned: not counting from the day on which they had their triumphal entry into their home cities, but from when they won the competition that made the triumph possible. I'm the one who writes "because of the *eiselastic* victory" opposite their names on the rolls, so I strongly suspect that it should be taken from the time when they εἰσήλασαν ["drove in," had their triumph]. The same men request *obsonia*[78] for a particular festival that you made *eiselastic*, although they won there before you did so. They say it is appropriate, since *obsonia* are not given to them for contests that ceased to be *eiselastic* at some point after their victories, so it should be given for those that have begun to be. This is also a fairly sticky point for me; there seems to be no logic in giving to someone who was not entitled to it at the time when he won. I therefore ask that you put an end to my doubts and deign to interpret the question by your own good will.

Trajan to Pliny

It seems to me that *eiselastic* honors should begin when someone εἰσήλασεν ["drives in"] to his own city. The *obsonia* for those contests which it has pleased me to make *eiselastic*, if they were not before, should not be given retroactively. For it cannot be in the athletes' interest if those who won at games which were *eiselastic* at the time and have ceased to be should stop receiving the *obsonia*. Moreover, when the state of a contest has been changed, we do not take back what they have already received.

---

[77] *Eiselastic* contests were those whose winners received a triumphal procession when they returned to their home cities; the word comes from a Greek word meaning "drive in," referring to the triumphal entry in a chariot.

[78] A pension or stipend, especially the one given to victors in the Greek festivals.

Inscriptions

ILS 5070 = CIL 3S.6829: from Antioch in Pisidia, date unknown.

Dedicated to Gaius Albucius Servius Firmus son of Gaius, aedile and *duovir*, who designated money in his will to provide for an athletic context to be held every year at the feast of the Moon.

ILS 5168 = CIL 6.10158, at Rome. Children's tombstones generally listed their ages to the day. It was unusual for children to perform; we do not know what kind of gymnastics these boys did.

Here lie three brothers, gymnasts: Euplus, who lived 5 years 8 months 13 days; Elenchius, who lived 1 year 7 months; Vincentius, who lived 5 years 9 months 29 days. Their foster-fathers and Basileus their father erected this for well-deserving children.

Animal Shows and Hunts

Animals were exhibited in the amphitheater as early as the third century BC, as we see in the selection from Plautus. As Rome explored and conquered more of the world, more exotic species were available to be exhibited; note the "African mice" here and the giraffe in the selection from Horace above. A wild animal hunt or *venatio* was also a popular spectacle. Finally, animals could be used to execute condemned criminals, who might be allowed to fight back or might be tied up, unable to resist. See also Martial's description of the opening *ludus* at the Flavian Amphitheater, below, and the correspondence between Cicero and Caelius about panthers in chapter 6.

Plautus, *Poenulus* 1008-1013

This selection comes from a play about a Carthaginian (Poenulus means "little Carthaginian" in Latin), a foreigner in Rome who cannot speak the language. It shows just how old was the custom of wild animal shows in the amphitheater.

> Milphio (a slave):
>> Hey you! You that talks funny! What are you doing in this city? What are you looking for?
>
> Hyanno (a Carthaginian):
>> Muphursa.
>
> Agorastocles (a young man, Milphio's master):
>> What's he say?
>
> Hyanno:　　Miuulechianna.
>
> Agorastocles: What's he doing?
>
> Milphio:　　Don't you hear him? He says he wants to give African mice[79] to the aediles for the procession at the *ludus*.
>
> Hyanno:　　Lechlachananilimniichot.

---

[79] "African mice" may be leopards; we do not know for certain.

Apuleius, *Golden Ass* 4.13

This selection comes shortly after Lucius has been turned into a donkey, when he has been taken in as a pack animal by a group of thieves. One of the thieves is telling a story, in which a *munus* figures incidentally.

We went up to Plataea, the next town. There the main gossip was about one Demochares who was going to put on a gladiatorial *munus*. He was one of the leading men in the town, very rich, and outstandingly generous, and he provided public spectacles worthy of his fortune. Who is clever enough or eloquent enough to find suitable words for all the different things he was preparing? Over here were gladiators famous for good hands, over there *venatores* who'd proven themselves dangerous, someplace else condemned criminals being fattened up as a banquet for the beasts. There were machines being put together, towers on wooden supports that looked just like one of the houses around the forum, all blooming with painted decorations, suitable containers for the beasts. And what a number of different beasts! He had taken particular care to provide suitable funeral monuments for those condemned criminals.

Gellius, *Attic Nights* 5.14

This story is well known and charming, but probably pure fiction.

Apion, known as "Plistonices," "the conqueror," was a man furnished with many books and very knowledgeable about science and matters Greek. His own books were famous: he wrote stories about nearly all the wonders ever seen or heard in Egypt. He was especially happy to talk about what he said he had heard or read himself, by way of showing off and vaunting the contents of his books. The following story, however, which he put in book 5 of his "Egyptian Wonders," is not one he heard or read; he asserts that he himself saw this with his own eyes in the city of Rome.

"In the Circus Maximus," Apion began, "a large and showy *venatio* was being given to the people. As I happened to be in Rome, I was in the audience. There were huge numbers of savage wild animals of unusual kinds and unusual ferocity. Among all these beasts the monstrous lions were the most admired, and among all the lions, one in particular stood out. This one lion captured everyone's attention by the size and speed of his body, the terrifying sound of his roar, and the rippling muscles and flowing mane of his neck.

"Among those brought in to fight these beasts was a slave given by an ex-consul; the name of this slave was Androclus. When the lion saw him from a distance, the beast suddenly stood still as if amazed, then slowly, calmly came up to the man as if he recognized him. He was wagging his tail gently in the time-honored way of fawning dogs; he rubbed up against the man's body and slowly licked his legs and hands. The man Androclus was breathless with fear at first, but as the wild animal continued to flatter him he calmed down and little by little began to observe the lion. Then you could see the man and the lion wishing each other joy, happy at a mutual recognition.

"At this amazing occurrence the crowd began to shout. Caesar summoned Androclus and asked why this exceedingly fierce lion had spared him alone. Then Androclus told his amazing story:

"'When my master was proconsul in the province of Africa, I was driven by his injustice and by daily beatings to run away. In order to hide safely from my master, who was after all the ruler of the area, I went away into isolated fields and deserts. My plan was, if I ran out of food, I would find another way to die. At noon, with the sun blazing in the sky, I came upon a remote, hidden cave, and concealed myself in there. Not much later, this lion came to the same cave. He was lame in one paw, which was bleeding, and he was moaning and whimpering from the pain of the wound.'

"At the first sight of the approaching lion, Androclus said, he was terrified. 'But when the lion came in,' he went on, 'into what appeared to be his home, he saw me hiding. He came gently up to me, raised his paw to show me, and appeared to be asking a favor. So I removed the huge thorn stuck in his paw, squeezed out the infected matter from the wound, then, becoming more confident, wiped away the blood and carefully dried it off. The lion, relieved by my medical ministrations, left his paw in my hands and sat quietly. For the next three years the lion and I lived in the same cave and lived the same life. He would hunt and bring the best parts of his prey back to the cave for me. As I had no fire, I would dry the meat in the sun, then eat it.

"'When I finally grew tired of the life of a wild animal, one day when the lion had gone out hunting I left the cave. I'd been on the road about three days when I was found and captured by soldiers and brought from Africa to my master, now in Rome. He at once had me condemned to capital punishment in the arena. I know that this lion has just thanked me for my doctoring and kindness.'"

Apion said that Androclus's story was written on placards and passed around to the people. By popular demand Androclus was pardoned and the lion was given to him. "Afterwards, he said, "we used to see Androclus with the lion on a little leash going all over the city to shops and taverns. People would give money to Androclus and flowers to the lion. Everyone would say, 'Here's the lion who's a man's friend and the man who's a lion's doctor.'"

Inscription

ILS 5147 = CIL 4.1989, from Pompeii. There were some famous *venatores*, though we know more individual gladiators.

There will be a *venatio* here on 28 August and Felix will fight bears.

Other Events

A *ludus* or *munus* could include other spectacles as well as competitions and *ludi scaenici*. Children and youths might dance, sing, or perform on horseback. Mythic re-enactments were popular. Some of these, as in the selection from Suetonius's *Life of Nero* above, were purely theatrical; more often, they were executions of criminals, as described in Martial's poems on the opening of the Flavian Amphitheater, below. Staged battles were also frequently a means of execution. Some emperors, like Caligula, prided themselves on inventing new kinds of spectacle; others, like Titus, were not so creative.

Virgil, *Aeneid* 5.545-603

The *ludus Troiae* or "Trojan game" was an equestrian drill performed by young men. Its origins are unknown, and by Virgil's time it was already traditional. Augustus made it a regular part of the spectacles he gave (see the selection from Suetonius's *Life of Augustus* in chapter 6). The funeral games for Anchises, Aeneas's father, in *Aeneid* book 5 are modeled on the funeral in *Iliad* 23, so they consist mainly of Greek-style competitions, but Virgil could not resist including a traditional Roman performance whose name apparently connects it with Aeneas and his Trojan followers who founded Rome. It is not known whether the name is actually from "Troy" or from a similar-sounding Etruscan word that may mean either "Troy" or "dancing."

When the archery was not quite over, father Aeneas called Periphas, Epytus's son, an older friend of young Iulus,[80] and said, "Go tell Ascanius, if he's got his troop of boys ready and formed up for their riding exercise, to bring them out here and present arms for his grandfather." He himself told everyone standing around to spread out and leave an open circle in the center.

The boys came in, shining in their parents' eyes just as much as the horses' trappings, and the rest of the Sicilian and Trojan youths murmured admiringly. The customary wreath of clipped leaves was on each one's head. Some of them carried pairs of cherry-wood spears with iron points, the rest had light quivers on their shoulders. Each one wore a chain of twisted gold around his neck.

Three squadrons of riders came behind three leaders; twelve boys, two by two, gleamed behind their leaders, each column with its trainer. Young Priam led the first troop of rejoicing boys, the son of Polites, named for his grandfather, and destined to make Italy great. A Thracian horse carried him, spotted with white on the front of his feet and on his high forehead.

Atys, Iulus's good friend, ancestor of the Latin Atius family, led the second troop. Iulus himself, the most beautiful of all, led the last column,

---

[80] Iulus, also called Ascanius, is Aeneas's son.

riding a Sidonian horse that fair Dido had given him as a memento and a token of affection. The rest of the boys rode Sicilian horses belonging to old king Acestes.

The watching Dardanians welcomed the nervous boys with applause and delight, and the boys found their parents in the crowd. When they had ridden happily around the whole circle of watching parents, Periphas gave the signal with a shout and a crack of his whip. They rode apart by pairs, splitting up their three columns, then when called back they turned around and raised their hostile weapons. Then they followed other paths, curving and re-curving across the area, weaving circles to one side and the other, imitating a battle. Now they expose their backs in flight, now enemies turn to their spears, now they make peace and ride side by side again. Like the Labyrinth in lofty Crete, which they say had a path woven of blind walls, an ambiguous trick of a thousand ways, in which an undiscovered error would destroy the tracks of your path so there would be no return, just so the Trojan boys wove and twisted their paths in the battle-game, like dolphins who divide the Carpathian from the Libyan by their swimming in the moist sea.

Ascanius revived this custom and contest, just as he had learned as a boy at Troy, and taught it to the early Latins when he put walls around Alba Longa, and the Albans taught their sons. Later great Rome received the custom and kept it in honor of her ancestors. It is now called the Trojan contest or Trojan battle.

And this concluded the funeral games for father Anchises.

Suetonius, *Life of Caligula*, sec. 18-20

Caligula lived from AD 12 to AD 41 and was emperor from 37 on. His real name was Gaius, but he was called Caligula, "Bootsie," because when he was a child he used to dress up in his father's military gear. No one *ever* called him Caligula to his face after he became emperor!

Caligula gave several gladiatorial *munera*, some in the amphitheater Statilius Taurus had built and some in the Saepta, bringing in troops of the best fighters from North Africa and Campania. He did not always preside at the spectacles himself, but sometimes made magistrates or his friends take charge of the *munus*. He gave frequent theatrical *ludi* of various kinds and in various places, even lighting up the whole city for nighttime spectacles. He scattered different kinds of things from the *missilia* and gave bread-baskets and food to every man. At one of these banquets, when a Roman knight was happily and greedily eating this food, Caligula sent him his own portion as well. He made a similarly appreciative senator a praetor before his time. Caligula gave many circus spectacles lasting from morning until night, including African-style *venationes* or the Trojan game, and for special occasions he would decorate the circus in red and green and use only charioteers from the senatorial order. He held some on short notice, as on one occasion when he was reviewing troops and several people on balconies nearby asked for a spectacle.

[Sec. 19] He thought up new kinds of spectacle that had never been done before. For example, he built a bridge joining the walls at Baiae to the fortification at Puteoli, a distance of about 36 miles, using merchant ships at anchor in a double row, with soil piled on them in the shape of the Appian Way. He went up and down this bridge for two days, on the first day riding a Falernian horse, crowned with oak leaves, carrying a sword and shield, and wearing a cloak woven with gold, on the second day in a chariot with a team of famous horses, with one of the Parthian hostages, a boy called Darius, beside him, accompanied by a troop of bodyguards and a group of friends in war-chariots. I know that many people thought Caligula had built such a bridge in deliberate imitation of Xerxes, who had made a bridge over the narrows of the Hellespont, an admirable feat. Others thought it was because the news of such an immense work would frighten the Germans and the Britons, whom he was intending to invade. But when I was a boy I heard my grandfather tell that the story going around the court was that Thrasylus the mathematician, concerned about who would succeed Tiberius and inclined to favor his real grandson, used to say "Gaius is no more likely to be emperor than to ride across the bay of Baiae on a horse."

[Sec. 20] Caligula also gave spectacles outside Rome: town *ludi* in Syracuse in Sicily and mixed games in Lugudunum in Gaul. In the latter place he included a contest in Greek and Latin eloquence, in which the prize for the winners was that the losers were made to speak in praise of them. Those who were the most unpleasant speakers were ordered to rub out their writings with a sponge or their tongues, unless they preferred to be reproached with the rod or dunked in the nearest river.

Life of Caligula, sec. 26-27

Here's Caligula's own idea of entertainment.

Caligula treated the other orders[81] with similar haughtiness and violence. When he was disturbed one night by noise from the people in the neighborhood of the circus, he had them all driven away with truncheons. In this disturbance more than 20 Roman knights and as many matrons were beaten, as were more other people than you could count. At the theater, to stir up trouble between the knights and the plebeians, he used to scatter gift-tokens too early (before the knights had arrived), so the lower classes would move into the knights' seats. At a gladiatorial *munus*, when the sun was blazing and the awnings had been put out, he would sometimes insist that they

---

[81] That is, the knights and the plebeians; the previous paragraph discussed his high-handed ways with the senate.

be taken off, and forbid anyone to leave. He would exhibit the cheapest, second-rate beasts and gladiators grown old and infirm. He would make men with physical disabilities fight, even if they were respectable, free citizens. And sometimes, he would close the granaries and announce that the people would starve.

[Sec. 27] In these ways he showed his natural cruelty. When cattle were being prepared to fatten up wild beasts for a *munus*, a fairly expensive business, Caligula decided to butcher criminals instead, and reviewing a row of them without looking at the record of the case, stood in the middle of the portico and ordered "take the ones from this bald one to that bald one." Someone had promised a gladiatorial show if he recovered from illness; Caligula held him to the vow and watched the fighting, nor did he let the man go until he won, and then only after he begged for it. He handed over another, who had vowed to commit suicide, to his slaves. They dragged him through the streets, crowned with sacred branches and the fillet of a priest or victim, to the old rampart, insisted the vow be fulfilled, and pushed him off. Caligula condemned many nobles to hard labor in the mines or on crews paving the roads, or to be given to the beasts, first branding them. Alternatively, he would put them in cages like animals, or cut them down the middle with a saw. These people were not all condemned for serious reasons, but rather for expressing an opinion about his shows, or because they would not swear by his spirit. He would force parents to be present at the punishment of their sons. When one tried to beg off because of poor health, he sent a litter to pick him up; he invited another to come directly from the spectacle of the punishment to a banquet where he made everyone laugh at him. There was a superintendent of *munera* and *venationes* whom he watched being whipped with chains for several days; he was not killed until the smell of rotting flesh became too offensive. There was a writer of Atellan farce whom he had burned alive on the sand in the middle of the amphitheater for some ambiguous lines in a play. When a Roman knight objected to being sent to the beasts and proclaimed his innocence, Caligula cut out his tongue and sent him back into the arena.

Life of Claudius, sec. 21

Claudius, born in 10 BC, succeeded Caligula in AD 41 and lived and reigned until 54.

Claudius gave distributions to the people frequently. His spectacles, too, were frequent and magnificent, not only the usual ones in the accustomed places, but new variants and revivals from the old days, and as almost no one had done before him. At the *ludi* for the dedication of Pompey's theater, which he restored after it burned down, he opened the proceedings from the tribune's position in the orchestra; he had first made a sacrifice in the temple behind the seats, then, when everyone else was seated and quiet, he came down through the center. He also gave the *ludi saeculares*,[82] as if Augustus had held them too early rather than waiting for the appropriate year, although in his own published inquiries into the question of timing he had said that Augustus had carefully worked out the correct year and put them back in order after a long interval. As a result, the herald's ritual announcement of games "that no one had ever seen or would ever see again" was rather funny, because there were people still alive who had seen the *ludi saeculares*, and some of the plays that had been produced the last time were to be produced again.

He frequently put on circus spectacles even in the Vatican, sometimes with a *venatio* after every five races. He adorned the circus with marble starting enclosures and golden turning posts; they had previously been made of tufa and wood respectively. He set aside reserved seats for the senators, who used to watch sitting mixed up with everyone else. In addition to races for four-horse chariots, he put on the Trojan game and African-style races, and exhibited a troop of praetorian cavalry under the leadership of tribunes and the prefect himself. There were also Thessalian knights, who drove wild bulls through the circus, wore them out, then jumped on them and brought them down by the horns.

Claudius gave many kinds of gladiatorial *munera* in many places: an annual *munus* in the camp of the praetorians without *venatio* or a great deal of ceremony; a regular *munus* in the Saepta; in the same place an unusual and rather short one which he called "the little basket" (*sportula*) because when it was first to be given he said that it was just like inviting the people to a spur-of-the-moment dinner party. There was no other kind of spectacle at which he was so relaxed and approachable, to the extent that when the gold pieces were being given to the winners, he would hold out his left hand and count them off on his fingers along with everyone else. By what he said and the questions he asked he would provoke merriment in the crowd, even calling them "lords," and making stiff, forced witticisms. For example, when the crowd called for Palumbus ["the Dove"], he promised to send him out, "if we can catch him." This next remark was really appropriate and timely: when the four sons of an *essedarius* pleaded for him to be released, to everyone's great pleasure he indulged the fellow, and put up a notice-board right there telling everyone "you, too, should have so many children; you see how they are a gladiator's nicest defense."

In the Campus Martius he staged the siege and pillaging of a town, imitating the war in Britain and the surrender of their kings, and he presided in a general's cloak. He held a naval battle on Lake Fucinus, before it was to be drained. But when the sailors shouted "Hail, *imperator*! Those about

---

[82] The *ludi saeculares*, or "hundred-year games," were supposed to be held every one hundred years. See the description of the *ludi saeculares* given by Augustus, below.

to die salute you!" he answered "Or not." After this, as if they had been pardoned, none of them was willing to fight. He hesitated for a long time, debating whether to have them all put to fire and the sword, but at last jumped out of his seat and ran around the shore of the lake, stumbling very badly, half warning and half exhorting them to fight. In this spectacle the Sicilian and the Rhodian fleets were represented as competing, 12 triremes at a time, spurred on by Triton, who rose up out of the lake on a mechanical platform and blew a silver horn.

Life of Titus, sec. 7

Titus was the son of Vespasian and was considered one of the "good" emperors, though he only reigned from 79 to 81. He was born in 41, the year Claudius succeeded Caligula. Martial's *Book of Spectacles* (see selections) is about the *munus* Titus gave to dedicate the Flavian Amphitheater, better known now as the Colosseum.

Titus gave parties that were pleasant rather than extravagant. Nevertheless, he was no less than his predecessors in generosity. When he had dedicated the amphitheater [the Colosseum], and rapidly built baths next to it, he gave a splendid, most lavish *munus* there. He also put on a naval battle in the place that had been used for this before, and in the same place had gladiators and in one day 5,000 beasts of every kind.

Martial, *Epigrams*

Martial was active during the reign of Titus. Many of his poems are about spectacles, *ludi*, and popular entertainment. These two describe punishments staged as re-enactments of the story of Mucius Scaevola. See also additional selections from Martial in chapter 6.

8.30

He who is now seen playing in Caesar's arena in the time of Brutus was the highest glory [i.e., Scaevola]. See how he endures the flames and enjoys his punishment; his brave hand rules the astonished fire! He is his own audience and loves the noble funeral of his right hand; it is nourished by the rites. For unless the punishment is taken away by someone unwilling, the left hand was also ready to go into the exhausted flames. After such a noble exhibition, it is painful to know what came before: it is enough for me to know that I have seen this hand.

10.25

In the arena this morning you saw Mucius, who put his hand in the fire. If he seemed to you brave and strong and long-enduring, then you have the brains of an Abderitan. Because when the *tunica molesta*[83] is standing

---

[83] *Tunica molesta* literally means "uncomfortable tunic." This tunic was soaked in pitch or some other flammable material, put onto a condemned criminal, then set on fire.

by and you're told, "Burn your hand," it's a greater accomplishment to say no.

Tertullian, *Apologeticus* 15.4-6

This book is Tertullian's main denunciation of the old Roman religion, which he considered inferior to Christianity. In this passage he describes the noontime events in the arena: the executions, often staged as scenes from myth.

You are clearly more religious in the amphitheater, where your gods dance around on human blood and the unclean leftovers of punishments, using criminals to serve up stories. Frequently the criminals act the parts of those very gods. At times, we have seen Attis castrated and becoming a god with Cybele,[84] and someone burning alive to become Hercules. We have laughed as among the playful mid-day cruelties Mercury examined the dead with a branding iron, and we have seen Pluto, Jupiter's brother, taking away the gladiators' corpses with an axe. Who could ask about all these things, one by one? If these acts disturb the honor of divinity, if they rub out the traces of majesty, they are held contemptible by those who do them just as by those for whom they are done.

Inscription

ILS 5173 = CIL 6.9797, at Rome. We do not know the exact nature of Ursus's ball game. The inscription is in verse, in the meter called "iambic senarius" that Plautus and Terence had used for plays. It appears from the names he mentions that Ursus lived early in the second century AD.

I am Ursus, the first Roman citizen to play with the glass ball in public, along with my company of ballplayers, to great applause and praise from the people, at Trajan's baths and Agrippa's and Titus's, and even Nero's, if you can believe it. Come, all you exultant ballplayers, and crown the statue of your friend with blooming roses and violets, green leaves, and soothing ointments. Come, lovers, and pour out dark wine, Falernian or Setinian or Caecubian, from the Emperor's own winecellar. Come sing in harmonious unison for old Ursus, merry and playful, a ballplayer and a rhetorician, who surpassed all his predecessors by his sensitivity and his highly subtle artistry. Now let an old man put some truth in the poem: even I was beaten, I admit, and not just once but many times, by my patron Verus, 3 times a consul. I freely let him call me a beginner.

---

[84] Cybele was a goddess whose worship was imported from Asia Minor. Originally, all the priests in her cult were eunuchs. Attis was a young man who, in a fit of religious madness, decided to become a priest of Cybele; when he regained his sanity, he was shocked at what he had done to himself. In some versions of the story he becomes a god and Cybele's consort; in others, notably Catullus, poem 63, he simply dies.

Complete Festivals

Suetonius, *Life of Julius Caesar*, sec. 39

This selection refers to the several triumphs Caesar celebrated in the 40s BC after his victories in Gaul and in his war against Pompey the Great.

Caesar gave various kinds of spectacles: a gladiatorial *munus*, *ludi* in every part of the city featuring actors in all languages, also circus races, athletic games, and a sea battle. At the *munus* in the forum, Furius Leptinus, of a praetorian family, fought with Quintus Calpenus, a former senator who pleaded cases in court. Children of princes from Asia and Bithynia did the pyrrhic dance. Decimus Laberius, a Roman knight, performed his mime at the *ludi*, and was paid 500 *sesterces* and a gold ring, then left the stage, went right through the orchestra, and took his seat among the knights.[85] The circus was lengthened at both ends and a moat was added around it; there young men from the very best families drove four-horse and two-horse chariots and did stunt-riding, jumping from one horse to another. There were two troops for the Trojan game, one of older boys and one of younger ones. There were five days of *venationes*, also a novel battle between two groups, with 500 foot soldiers, 20 elephants, and 300 cavalry fighting at a time. So that they could take a break during the battle, the turning-posts were taken away and in their place camps were set up at opposite ends of the amphitheater. The athletes competed for three days in a temporary stadium built near the Campus Martius. The naval battle took place in a small lake dug out of the Lesser Codeta. Triremes and quadriremes from the Tyrian and Egyptian fleets fought a large number of battles. So many people thronged to all these spectacles that a lot of the visitors from out of town had to stay in tents pitched in the streets. Many people were trampled or killed by the crowd, including two senators.

Inscription

ILS 5050 = CIL 6.32323, at Rome, in the Campus Martius. This inscription describes Augustus's *Ludi Saeculares* of 17 BC. Note that most of the text describes the sacrifices and prayers; although the sporting events are mentioned, the most important thing about the festival is its religious nature. The repeated mentions of "those books" refer to the Sibylline oracles. The song written by Horace, to be sung by 27 boys and 27 girls, still exists and is called his "Carmen Saeculare." Because the stone is broken, we pick up the account in the middle.

On the following night in the field by the Tiber the emperor Caesar Augustus sacrificed 9 female lambs to the Moirae[86] following the Achaean

---

[85] The gold ring was the badge of a knight. Strictly, members of the upper classes were not supposed to perform, so Laberius temporarily relinquished his rank, then took back his ring and his seat after the mime was over.

[86] These are the "Fates," here called by their Greek name.

ritual, and 9 female goats in the same way. The animals were to be consumed by the fire, and he prayed in this way:

"Moirae! As is written for you in those books, and so that everything may be for the best for the Roman people the Quirites, let these 9 female lambs and 9 female goats be a sacrifice to you. I pray and beseech that you increase the power and greatness of the Roman people the Quirites in war and at home; that you always watch over the Latin power; that you grant safety, eternal victory, and well-being to the Roman people the Quirites; that you support the Roman people the Quirites and keep the legions and the republic of the Roman people the Quirites safe; that you willingly be propitious to the Roman people the Quirites, the college of *quindecemviri*, me, my house, and my family; and that you be accepting of this sacrifice of 9 female lambs and 9 female goats suitable for sacrificing. Accept therefore the sacrifice of this female lamb and be willingly propitious to the Roman people the Quirites, the college of *quindecemviri*, me, my house, and my family."

When the sacrifice was finished that night, the *ludi* began on a stage without a theater and without seats. 110 matrons designated by the *quindecemviri* held a divine banquet, and two seats were set up there for Juno and Diana.

On the first of June on the Capitoline hill the Emperor Caesar Augustus sacrificed a suitable bull to Jupiter the Best and Greatest, and Marcus Agrippa did the same, and they prayed thus:

"Jupiter, Best and Greatest! As it is written for you in those books, and so that everything may be for the best for the Roman people the Quirites, let this beautiful bull be a sacrifice to you. I pray and beseech you" and the rest as above.

At the altar were Caesar, Agrippa, Scaevola, Sentius, Lollius, Asinius Gallus, Rebilus.

Then the Latin *ludi* began in a wooden theater built in the field by the Tiber. Mothers of families held a divine banquet in the same way. The *ludi* that began that night continued throughout the festival, and the following proclamation was made by the *quindecemviri*:

"Whereas it is a good custom, known from many examples, that whenever there is just cause for public rejoicing, it is appropriate to limit women's mourning, and whereas the diligent observation of this custom at a time of such solemn and sacred *ludi* seems to affect both the honor of the gods and our mindfulness of their worship, we therefore decree it to be our duty to announce to the women that they limit their mourning."

That night at the Tiber the Emperor Caesar Augustus sacrificed to Ilithyia, goddess of childbirth, 9 liba, 9 popana, and 9 phthois,[87] and he prayed in this way:

---

[87] These are three different kinds of cakes or pastries.

"Ilithyia! As it is written for you in those books, and so that everything may be for the best for the Roman people the Quirites, let these 9 popana and 9 liba and 9 phthois be a sacrifice to you. I pray and beseech you" and the rest as above.

On the second of June on the Capitoline hill the Emperor Caesar Augustus sacrificed a cow to Queen Juno, and Marcus Agrippa did the same, and they prayed this way:

"Queen Juno! As it is written for you in those books, and so that everything may be for the best for the Roman people the Quirites, let this beautiful cow be a sacrifice for you. I pray and beseech you" and the rest as above.

Then he gave directions to 110 married women, mothers of families, in these words:

"Queen Juno, these married women pray on their knees that you increase the power and greatness of the Roman people the Quirites in war and at home; that you always watch over the Latin power; that you grant safety, eternal victory, and well-being to the Roman people the Quirites; that you support the Roman people the Quirites and keep the legions and the republic of the Roman people the Quirites safe; that you willingly be propitious to the Roman people the Quirites, the *quindecemviri* in charge of the sacrifice, and us. These things we, 110 married mothers of families of the Roman people the Quirites, on our knees seek and pray for."

At the altar were Marcus Agrippa, ... [the other names are lost].

Ludi were held as on the previous day.

That night at the Tiber, the Emperor Caesar Augustus sacrificed a pregnant sow to Mother Earth and prayed this way:

"Mother Earth! As it is written for you in those books, and so that everything may be for the best for the Roman people the Quirites, let this suitable pregnant sow be a sacrifice for you. I pray and beseech you" and the rest as above.

The matrons held a divine banquet on this day in the same way as before.

On the third day of June on the Palatine hill the Emperor Caesar Augustus and Marcus Agrippa sacrificed 9 liba, 9 popana, and 9 phthois to Apollo and Diana and prayed thus:

"Apollo, as it is written for you in those books and so that all may be for the best for the Roman people the Quirites, let these 9 popana, 9 liba, 9 phthois be a sacrifice for you. I pray and beseech you" and the rest as above. "Apollo, since I have prayed well to you by giving these popana, accept therefore the libation with these liba and be willingly propitious." The same with the phthois; the same words to Diana.

When the sacrifice was complete, 27 designated boys whose fathers and mothers were still alive, and as many girls, sang a song, and in the same way on the Capitoline. Quintus Horatius Flaccus composed the song.

The *quindecemviri* were present: the Emperor Caesar Augustus, Marcus Agrippa, Quintus Lepidus, Potitus Messalla, Gaius Stolo, Gaius Scaevola, Gaius Sosius, Gaius Norbanus, Marcus Cocceius, Marcus Lollius, Gaius Sentius, Marcus Strigo, Lucius Arruntius, Gaius Asinius, Marcus Marcellus, Decimus Laelius, Quintus Tubero, Gaius Rebilus, Messala, Messallinus.

When the theatrical *ludi* ended, next to the place where the sacrifices were made on the previous nights and near the theater and the stage, turning-posts were erected and chariot races were held. Potitus Messalla started off the equestrian acrobats. The following proclamation was made by the *quindecemviri*:

"We have added seven days of honorary *ludi* to the solemn *ludi*. On the fifth of June Latin *ludi* will begin in the wooden theater near the Tiber at the second hour, Greek theatrical *ludi* in Pompey's theater at the third hour, Greek city *ludi* in the theater at the circus Flaminius at the fourth hour."

The next day, the fourth of June, was a break in the festival, and on the fifth of June began the Latin *ludi* in the wooden theater, Greek theatrical *ludi* in Pompey's theater, and Greek city *ludi* in the theater at the circus Flaminius.

On the eleventh of June the *quindecemviri* made the following proclamation: "On the twelfth of June we will give a *venatio* and will begin circus *ludi*."

On the twelfth of June there was a procession of boys[88] ... and Marcus Agrippa started off the chariots.

All these things were done by the *quindecemviri*: the Emperor Caesar Augustus, Marcus Agrippa, Gnaeus Pompeius, Gaius Stolo, Marcus Marcellus, ... [the other names are lost].

Martial, *Book of Spectacles*

These are the poems of the *Book of Spectacles*, describing the first *ludi* held in the Flavian Amphitheater. Because the amphitheater was built on the land Nero had used for his Colossus and his Golden House, Martial often refers to the replacement of Nero's private pleasure palace with a public entertainment center, for example in poem 2. Most of the events described here are public executions in the form of dramatizations of episodes from myth or Roman history, but there are also *venationes* and a sea-battle.

1. May barbarous Memphis be silent about the marvels of the pyramids; may Assyrian labor not boast about Babylon; may the soft Ionians not be praised for the temple of Diana of the Three Ways; may the altar crowded

---

[88] Perhaps this was the Trojan game.

with horns keep Delos secret; may the Carians not praise the tomb of Mausolus to excess as it hangs in the empty air. Every work yields to the Amphitheater of Caesar, and Fame shall speak of this one work instead of all the others.

2. Here where the sky-high colossus sees the stars close up and tall scaffolding grows in the middle of the road, the hateful halls of a wild king used to gleam, the one house that stood in all the blazing city. Here where the awesome bulk of the wonderful Amphitheater is going up, there used to be Nero's ponds. Here where we marvel at baths, rapidly built, a haughty field once took away wretched people's homes. Where the Claudian colonnade casts a long shadow, there used to be the innermost part of a courtyard, now gone. Rome has been given back to Rome. Under your direction, Caesar, what was once the master's delight now belongs to the people.

3. What nation is so far away or so barbarous that it sends no spectators to your city, Caesar? The Rhodopeian farmer comes from Orpheus's Mount Haemon; the Sarmatian shepherd comes on the mare whose milk he drinks; and he who drinks from the source of the Nile, and he whom great Tethys's waves carry. The Arab hurries here, the Sabaeans too, and the Cilicians arrive wet with their clouds. The Sicambrians come with their hair tied up in buns, and the Ethiopians with their different twisted hairstyle. The people speak with one voice in many different languages: you are the true Father of everyone's country.

4. The solemn crowd of informers is the enemy of peace and placid quiet. It always used to stir up the wretched people. It has been led away with placards, and the arena cannot compass all those who would harm.

5. The informer has been informed of his own exile from Rome. You may count this all to the credit of the Prince.

6. Believe in Pasiphae joined to the Cretan bull: we have seen it; the old story is believable. Nor, O Caesar, should antiquity be amazed at itself: whatever Fame sings of, the arena presents to you.

7. Caesar, it is not enough that Mars serve you with his unconquered arms—Venus herself serves you too.

8. Noble Fame used to sing of the work of Hercules and the lion brought down in the vast Nemean valley. May the ancient story be silent: after your *munera*, O Caesar, we have seen these deeds done by a woman's hand.

9. Just as Prometheus, tied to his Scythian rock, fed the bird constantly pecking at his breast, so Laureolus, hanging on a genuine cross, offered his naked guts to a Caledonian bear. The torn-off limbs were still alive and dripping, but in the entire body there was no body. He had a suitable punishment: the wicked man had pricked his master's throat with a sword, or, crazy, had stolen the hidden gold from a temple, or had put

savage torches up to you, Rome. The criminal surpasses the faults of the old rumors: what was once a play is now a punishment.

10. Daedalus, as you were ripped by the Lucanian bear, you must have wished you had your wings!

11. The rhinoceros was shown off for you throughout the arena, O Caesar, and offered even more battles than he had promised. O what a terrible rage burned him as he lowered his head! Such a bull he was that a bull was a football for him.

12. A faithless lion had hurt his master with his ungrateful mouth and dared to defile the familiar hands. Yet he paid a penalty worthy of such a crime: he who had never felt the lash felt weapons. What manners are appropriate for men under such an emperor who orders the nature of wild beasts to be gentler?

13. As a bear turned hastily this way and that on the bloody sand, he got tangled in bird-lime and lost escape. Now the brilliant spears must stop and cover their points and the lance must not fly, shaken by the twist of the hand. May the *venator* catch beasts from the empty air, if it pleases Caesar that they be caught by the bird-catcher's art.

14. As Diana presided over Caesar's violent contest, a light spear pierced a sow heavy with young. A piglet leapt from the wretched mother's wound. Cruel Lucina, what kind of birthing was this? She would have wanted to die from more weapons' wounds if the sad way would lie open for all the litter. Who denies that Bacchus came forth in his mother's death? Believe a divinity was thus born, since so was a beast.

15. Struck by a grim weapon and pierced with wounds, the mother sow at once gave life and gave it up. How sure was the hand with the well-balanced steel! I believe it was the hand of Lucina herself. In her death the sow know both aspects of Diana: the birth eased by the one, the death by the other.

16. A wild sow, weighted down by the ripeness of her womb, gave birth, made a parent by a wound, nor did the newborn lie still but ran off as its mother died. What a clever surprise!

17. The highest glory of your reputation, Meleager, was the death of the boar, and it was not as much as Carpophorus the *bestiarius* had. He lodged his hunting-spears in a charging bear, a leader from the citadel of polar Arctois; he laid out a huge lion who would have done Hercules credit; and he stretched out a swift leopard with a wound. Thus he could have both praises and prizes.

18. A bull was snatched away from the middle of the arena to the stars. This was the work not of art but of duty.

19. A bull once conveyed Europa through his brother's sea, but now a bull has carried Alcides [Hercules] to the stars. Now, Fame, compare

Caesar's bull and Jupiter's: they carried an equal burden, but one carried his higher.

20. How dutifully the elephant kneels and adores you, Caesar, though just now he was such an object of fear for the bull. He does not do this on orders, and no teacher has schooled him. Believe me, even he recognizes our god.

21. A tigress, a rare glory from a Caspian mountain, who would often lick her fearless master's hand, tore a wild lion violently to pieces with her savage teeth—a new thing, not known to any era. While she lived in the high forests she never dared do such a thing, but since she has been with us she has become more fierce.

22. The bull, who was just goaded all round the arena by flames, grabbed balls and tossed them to the stars. He fell at last, caught by a tusk, thinking he could play so easily with the elephant.

23. When this side wanted Myrinus and that side wanted Triumphus, Caesar promised one of them for each side. There was no better way to resolve the comical case. O sweet cleverness of an unconquered emperor!

24. Whatever they say was shown to Rhodope in Orpheus's theater, Caesar, your arena has shown to you. Rocks crawled and trees miraculously ran, just as in the Hesperides' grove. All kinds of beasts, wild and domestic together, were there, and many a bird hovered over the bard, but he himself fell, mauled by an unappreciative bear. This was the only thing that contradicted the story.

25. Are we surprised that the earth suddenly opens up and sends Orpheus out? The bear comes from buried Eurydice.

26. While the fearful masters were taunting the rhinoceros and the great beast's anger was growing stronger, they despaired of the battle they'd promised—but at last the animal's old fury came back. He tossed a weighty bear on his twin horns as a bull tosses balls up in the air. The strong right hand of Carpophorus struck clean and true with his hunting spear. He brought twin bull-calves easily under the yoke; to him the fierce buffalo and bison yielded. When the lion fled he ran straight into the weapons. Go on then, crowd, blame the slow delay.

27. If you are a late arrival from a distant shore and this was your first day at the sacred *munus*, do not be deceived by the ships and the waves like the sea. Just now this was dry land. Don't you believe me? Look, while the waters tire Mars. In a little while, you will say "just now, this was the sea."

28. Stop being surprised that the nocturnal wave spared you, Leander: it was Caesar's wave.

29. When bold Leander sought his sweet love and, tired, was oppressed by the swelling sea, this is what the poor boy said to the threatening waves:

"Spare me now, I'm in a hurry; drown me when I come back."

30. A chorus of Nereids played in all the waves and variously arranged themselves to make pictures on the gentle water. The trident threatened with its straight tooth, the anchor with its curved one. We believed in the oar, and we believed in the boat, and the shining of the Twins' star, welcome to sailors, and the billowing and obvious folds of the broad sail. Who discovered such arts in the flowing waves? Thetis either taught or learned these games.

31. While Priscus and Verus prolonged their contest, and the fortunes of battle were equal for each of them, there was a great and frequent clamor for *missio* for both of them. But Caesar himself obeyed his law: that they contend, shieldless, until a finger was raised. He did permit himself to give them platters of money frequently. At last they found an end to their well-matched match: they fought as equals, they conceded as equals. Caesar sent each one the *rudis* and a victory palm, prize for inborn excellence. It has never happened under any emperor but you, Caesar, that two men contended and each was the victor.

32. Caesar, if bygone centuries had had a Carpophorus, the barbarian land would not have feared the Parthaonian beast, nor Marathon the bull, nor leafy Nemea the lion, nor Arcas the Maeadian boar. When he took up arms, the hydra would have had a single death, and the Chimaera would have been struck down once and for all. He could have yoked the fire-breathing bulls without the Colchian woman, and he could have conquered either of Pasiphae's beasts. If the sea-monster is to have a return engagement, he could save Hesione and Andromeda single-handed. The glory of Hercules may be counted in 12 labors—but it is a greater thing to have conquered wild beasts 20 at a time.

33. When the agitated antelope fled the swift Molossians, contriving various measures to delay her fate, she came and stood at Caesar's feet as a suppliant, and the dogs did not touch their prize. When the Prince saw what she wanted, he gave it to her as a gift. Caesar's will is divine, his power is sacred—believe it! Wild animals have never learned to lie.

34. Augustus accomplished the feat of gathering fleets here and stirring up the waves with naval battle. What part is this of *our* Caesar? Thetis and Galatea saw beasts in the waters that they did not recognize. Triton saw chariots racing through the water, kicking up seafoam like clouds of dust, and thought he saw his master's horses. While Nereus was preparing a wild battle for fierce ships, he shivered at the footsoldiers coming across the liquid water. Whatever is visible in the Circus and the Amphitheater, Caesar, the rich waves offer to you. Let Fucinus be silent, and nasty Nero's swamp: the ages will know this sea battle alone.

35. Pardon the speed of these poems: one who hastens to please you, Caesar, does not deserve your displeasure.

36. To yield to one greater in virtue is the second-best reputation. Great indeed is the victory if the lesser man wins.

Statius, *Silvae* 1.6

This poem describes the Saturnalia celebration given by Domitian.

Father Phoebus, grave Pallas, Muses: go away, take a break. We will call you back at the start of January. It's Saturn I want at my side, freed from his fetters, and December, full of neat wine, and cheeky, laughing Joke and Wit, while I tell about happy Caesar's joyful day and wine-rich banquet.

Aurora had barely begun to rise when already sweet things were raining from the *missilia* like dew spread by the east wind. Something noble from the Pontic nut trees, or dates from Idyme's mountains, the plums that good Damascus grows on its branches, the figs that ripen at Ebusus or Caunus—all these fall abundantly, free for the taking. Little people-cakes, sweetmeats, pastry from Amerina—not overcooked! –, wine-flavored wedding-cakes, and stuffed dates from hidden palms were falling. None of the cloudy Hyades or the unrestrained Pleiades ever poured such a storm on the earth as the hail that the clear winder sky loosed upon the Roman people in the amphitheater. Jupiter may send clouds all over the world and threaten the broad fields with rain, if only our own Jupiter will keep up *this* rain.

Then, look! All through the audience comes another crowd, no smaller than the one in the seats, and especially attractive and well-dressed. Some bring up bread baskets, gleaming white napkins, and fancier foods. Others dispense relaxing wine all around; you would think they were all the cupbearer of Mount Ida.[89] Blessed one, since you nourish the circle where the best people sit, and the other citizens in togas, and everyone else, haughty grain-goddess Annona knows nothing of this day. Go back and compare past ages, O Antiquity, even the golden age of Saturn: wine did not flow so freely then, nor did the harvest take over the end of the year. Every class eats at the same table: children, women, plebeians, knights, senators: freedom has relieved respect. Even you yourself are here at the banquet like one of our company. Which of the gods has leisure for this, or would undertake such a thing? Now everyone, poor or well-off, prides himself on sharing a meal with our leader.

As the crowd murmurs at its new delights, they also take pleasure in watching. There stand the weaker sex, untrained with swords, nonetheless taking on a manly fight. You would think Thermodontian Amazons were mixing it up at the Don or the wild Phasis. Over here, see the bold order of dwarfs, whom nature has made short and gnarly. They deal out wounds

---

[89] This is Ganymede, the beautiful young man whom Jupiter took up to heaven to serve his wine.

and threaten death at each other's hands—such hands! Father Mars and bloodthirsty Virtue laugh, and cranes,[90] intending to come down for plunder, threaten the fierce fighters.

Now, as the shadows of night come quickly on, what excitement there is at the rich *sparsio*! Here enter girls, easily bought, and here everyone recognizes the pleasing shape or approved art of the theater. Here Lydian girls, nicely filled out, applaud in a group; there cymbals and Spanish bells ring; there crowds of Syrians make noise; here are the theater people, there those who exchange ordinary sulfur for broken glass.[91]

Among all these people suddenly huge clouds of birds fall from the stars—flamingos from the holy Nile, pheasants from the wild Phasis, and guinea-hens the Numidians catch when the wind blows moist from the south. There are far more birds than people, and everyone takes pleasure in filling the folds of his toga and receiving new riches. They raise countless shouts to the stars, calling out for the Emperor's Saturnalia and the sweet favor of their Master—but this alone Caesar declines to permit: we may not call him Master.

Dark-blue night had barely begun to spread over the sky when a shining fire came down into the middle of the sand among the deep shadows, brighter than Ariadne's Gnosian crown. The sky shone with fire and dark night was not allowed to do anything. Lazy Quiet and idle Sleep, seeing this, quickly fled to other cities. Who can sing of the spectacles, the unrestrained laughter, the parties, the free banquets, the broad river of wine? Now even I flag and, drunk on your wine, am dragged off at last to sleep.

For how many years will this day go on! The holy festival will never grow old, so long as the Latian mountains, father Tiber, your Rome, and the Capital you have given back to the world will stand.

Inscriptions

ILS 5050a = CIL 6.32327. This very fragmentary stone records preparations for the *ludi saeculares* celebrated by Septimius Severus and his son and co-emperor Caracalla in AD 204.

On 15 April the emperors sent the following letter: "Emperor Caesar Lucius Septimius Severus and Emperor Caesar Marcus Aurelius Antoninus Pius, Augusti, to the college of *quindecemviri*, greetings. If it seems best to you, on 25 May next, assemble on the Palatine in the temple of Apollo to determine by lot who should distribute incense to the people and from which locations. Farewell, our dearest colleagues."

"Pompeius Rusonianus, lawful head of the college of *quindecemviri*,

---

[90] Cranes were the traditional enemies of Pygmies, as mentioned for example in Homer's *Iliad* 3.3.

[91] These men are giving out sulfur matches in exchange for glass that can be recycled.

and the emperors Caesar Lucius Septimius Severus and Marcus Aurelius Antoninus Pius, Augusti, to the college of *quindecemviri*, greetings. If you are deliberating about the days and nights on which the *ludi* should be held, ..., and at the same time what incense the matrons should use when praying to the gods, we will make the decision. Farewell, our dearest colleagues."

"Pompeius Rusonianus, lawful head of the college of *quindecemviri*, ... On 25 May the college assembled on the Palatine in the temple of Apollo to determine by lot who should distribute incense to the people and from which locations. Present were the Emperor Caesar Lucius Septimius Severus Pius Pertinax Augustus Arabicus Adiabaticus Parthicus Maximus, the Emperor Caesar Marcus Aurelius Antoninus Pius Augustus, Nonius Mucianus, Pollienus Auspex, Manilius Fuscus, Cocceius Vibianus, Atulenus Rufinus, Aiacius Modestus, Fabius Magnus, Pompeius Rusonius the leader, Crescens Calpurnianus, Cassius Pius Marcellinus the quaestor-designate, Ulpius Soter the consul-designate, Venidius Rufus the curator for water and sewers, Fulvius Granianus priest of Augustus ... [other names missing]. The tokens were inspected and put into the urn, and the lot was cast. On the Palatine at the monument to our Augusti in the courtyard of the temple of Apollo ... and Salvius Tuscus; ... near the Roman square; ... in front of the temple of .... [names of *quindecemviri* and places of assignment missing]"

ILS 5055 = CIL 10.7295, from Panormo, date unknown. This is the middle part of a three-stone monument honoring someone whose name is lost.

He served as curator of the calendar with the greatest good faith. At the same time, he was also curator of the calendar for the Port, a task he carried out with the greatest diligence. With the Emperor's permission, he put on a praiseworthy *munus*. When he received what he wanted, he gave a most welcome spectacle to all the citizens. The people had many hours of pleasure in the theater. In the afternoon, everyone happily moved from there to the arena, where they were amazed at the magnificent spectacle of all kinds of herbivores and many beasts from the east. With the emperor's permission, specially obtained, he provided a lavish banquet for all his fellow citizens. Because of these freely-given pleasures, and from a desire to bring greater honor to this best of men, the people voted by centuries to erect a statue of him in a chariot.

ILS 5072 = CIL 8S.11998, from somewhere in Africa. The date and the name of the honoree are unknown.

... and when he became flamen he promised 2,000 *sesterces* for this great honor. He made a dedication with the increased money and on that occasion gave gifts to the decuriones, a banquet to the entire population, and a gymnastic contest; at the same spectacle he also showed boxers, chariot races, and plays.

Chapter 5

Women and Sports

These texts focus on women, family life, and sexuality as connected with sports, especially with gladiators. Normally women did not compete, although they were occasionally brought into the arena for a novelty. They did go to the theater, the circus, and the arena, however, and it was a standard stereotype that they found gladiators attractive. See also Martial, *Book of Spectacles*, Statius, *Silvae* 1.6, all in ch. 4, about women fighting in the arena, the selections from Ovid in chapter 3 about women watching the races at the circus, and the mention of women gladiators in the selection from Suetonius's life of Domitian in ch. 6.

Propertius, *Elegies* 3.14

Here Propertius fantasizes about athletic women. Sparta was a city in Greece with a strong tradition of militarism; everyone in Sparta, male and female, was expected to keep in fighting shape. The customs described here are typical of the seventh—fourth centuries BC; by the first century BC, when Propertius lived, Sparta was under Roman rule like the rest of Greece and was becoming Romanized.

Sparta, we are amazed at the rules of your wrestling schools, and particularly at the young women athletes: for your girls, there is no shame in working out, naked among the men wrestling. The ball, thrown swiftly from hand to hand, confuses the spectators; the hoop rattles as the hooked stick rolls it along; a woman stands in the dust at the far turning-post, or gets hurt in the harsh pancration.[92] Now she happily straps boxing-gloves to her hands, now the heavy discus whirls as she throws it. Her horse's hooves pound the ring; she girds a sword to her snow-white side and covers her maidenly head with hollow bronze; and then she follows the local hounds over the ridges of Mt. Taygetus, getting snow in her hair. She is like the warrior Amazons, who bathe with nude breasts in the waters of Thermodon, or like Castor and Pollux on the sands of Eurota, the one a victorious boxer, the other a horseman. Helen, they say, took up arms along with them, and did not blush to bare her breast before her divine brothers.

---

[92] The pancration was a Greek combat sport in which almost anything was permitted, except biting and eye-gouging.

Thus the Spartan law forbids the separation of lovers, and allows a man to be at his mistress's side in public places. Girls are not locked away, timid and under guard, and a man does not have to fear punishment. You can talk to her yourself and plead your case with no middle-men, no rejection, no long wait. Rich purple clothes do not seduce wandering eyes, and there is no fussing with perfumed hair.

The Roman woman, on the other hand, goes around in a huge crowd—you can't get anywhere near her, can't find out what she's really like or find a way to talk to her. A lover is quite in the dark. Rome, if you would adopt the rules of Spartan wrestling, you would be even dearer to me.

Petronius, *Satyricon* sec. 126

A slave describes her mistress for the narrator's benefit. The mistress, seated in the orchestra with the senatorial class, looks beyond the knights' 14 rows to the lower classes in the higher seats.

Since you say you're a slave, a commoner, you'll set her on fire with passion. There are some women, you know, that get hot for low-lifes, and they don't get aroused unless it's a slave's tunic they're tucking up. The arena turns others on, either covered with dust for fighting or given over to a theatrical show. My lady's one of those: from the orchestra she jumps over 14 rows and looks way up among the plebeians for what she wants.

Juvenal, *Satire* 6, 76-81, 98-113, 246-267

In satire 6, by far the longest of the group, Juvenal discusses women's faults. One of these faults, according to him, is an excessive attraction to gladiators. In two of these passages, Juvenal describes women who have adulterous affairs with gladiators. In the third, he describes a woman who wants to be a gladiator herself. For Juvenal, and probably for most Romans, the idea of a woman gladiator was preposterous because fighting was considered unfeminine and unwomanly.

76-81: You have taken a wife by whom Echion the cithara-singer will become a father, or Glaphyrus, or Ambrosius who accompanies choruses on the aulos.[93] Let's put up long reviewing stands in all the narrow street and decorate the doorposts with laurel, Lentulus, because your noble son, under the canopy in his tortoise-shell crib, is the very image of Euryalus the *murmillo*.

98-113: If her husband orders her, it's hard to travel on board ship: the bilge-water smells bad and she's dizzy with seasickness. But if she's following her lover, her stomach's fine. The one vomits all over her husband, the other eats with the sailors, runs up and down the deck, and

---

[93] An *aulos* was a Greek musical instrument, related to the modern oboe.

loves to pull on the rough ropes. So what kind of body does Eppia burn for? Whose youth has caught her eye? What does she see for which she puts up with being called "Gladiator Girl"? Her dear Sergius has already begun to shave his throat, like an older fellow, and to anticipate retirement with his cut-up arm. There are lots of ugly things on his face, like a huge wart on the middle of his nose, right where the helmet rubs it, and foul stuff always dripping from his eyes. But he was a gladiator. That makes him a Hyacinth; for that, she prefers him to her sons, her country, her sister, and her husband. It's the sword that they love. This same Sergius, when he gets his *rudis*,[94] begins to look like Veiento.[95]

246-267: Who doesn't know about the purple athletes' cloaks and the ladies' wrestling ointment? Who hasn't seen the wounds on the *palus*, which they've gouged with the *rudis* and beaten with the shield? She goes through all the exercises and is quite worthy to blow the trumpet at the Floralia, though she's a matron—unless she has bigger ideas and wants to appear in the real arena. What decency can a woman show wearing a helmet, when she leaves her own sex behind? She wants to be strong like a man, but does not want to turn into a man: after all, we men have such little pleasure. Such an honor, if her husband holds a yard sale, to auction off her *balteus*, *manicae*, helmet-crests, and a Samnite-style greave. Or if a different kind of fighting moves her, you'll be happy that she sells her Thracian greaves. There are women who sweat in a delicate, embroidered robe, who broil in even a light silk dress. See how she grunts as she repeats the blows the trainer shows her, how she's weighted down by the helmet, what thick bark bandages wrap her knees. Then laugh when she puts down her weapons and sits down to piss. Tell me, descendants of Aemilius Lepidus, of blind Metellus, of Maximus Gurges, of Quintus Fabius, of all ancient and famous Romans, what gladiator's girl would ever dress up like this? When did Asylius's girl ever get out of breath at the *palus*?

Tacitus, *Annals* 15.32

Women gladiators were not just a fantasy of the satirists.

In the same year Nero Caesar granted the Latin rights to the people of the province of Maritime Alps. He put the knights' seats in front of the plebs at the circus; up to this time they had sat all mixed together, because the *Lex Roscia*[96] only dealt with the fourteen rows. That year saw gladiator spectacles as magnificent as any prior year, but many distinguished

[94] The *rudis* was a wooden practice sword. When a gladiator retired, he was given a *rudis*, perhaps as a symbolic replacement for the real sword he would no longer need. Hence to "get his *rudis*" means to retire.
[95] "Veiento" might be the name of Eppia's husband, or might be a proverbial name for any ugly old man.
[96] The *Lex Roscia*, of 67 BC, was the main law making rules for seating in the theater and the amphitheater. See selections in chapter 6 for more about this law and its effects.

women and senators were disgraced in the arena.

Plutarch, *Moralia* 1099a-d

Plutarch here uses the behavior of gladiators as an example for other people. Because gladiator fights went on until one of the fighters killed the other, every gladiator had to be prepared to die.

What must be said about the exceptionally good? Suppose an ordinary person was about to die, and his master—a god or a king—could give him one more hour, to be spent in some good or profitable pursuit before death. In that hour, who would choose to meet Lais and drink Ariousian wine with her instead of killing Archias to set the Thebans free?[97] No one, I think. For I see gladiators, those who are not entirely savage but Greeks, when they are about to be sent into the arena and all sorts of expensive food is put before them, preferring to entrust their wives to their friends' protection and free their slaves rather than to gratify their stomachs.

Inscriptions

Tombstones of gladiators often open a window onto their family lives. Many had wives and children.

ILS 5090 = CIL 6.10195, at Rome

Sacred to the memory of Marcus Antonius Niger, veteran Thraex, who lived 38 years, fought 18 times. Flavia Diogenis erected this at her own expense for a well-deserving husband.

ILS 5095 = CIL 12.3323, at Nemausis

Beryllus, *essedarius*, freed after 20 fights, born a Greek, 25 years old. Nomas his wife erected this for a well-deserving husband.

ILS 5104 = CIL 6.10177 and 6.33977, at Rome

Sacred to the memory of Marcus Ulpius Felix, veteran *murmillo*, lived 45 years old, Tungerian by birth. Ulpia Syntyche, freedwoman, for her sweetest and well-deserving husband, and Justus his son erected this.

ILS 5107 = CIL 5.2884, at Patavia

Sacred to the memory of Purricina Iuvenus, *provocator*, erected by his wife for a well-deserving husband. He lived 21 years, was in the gladiator *ludus* 4 years, fought 5 times.

ILS 5115 = CIL 5.5933, at Milan

Sacred to the memory of Urbicus, *secutor*, left-handed, Florentine by birth, who fought 13 times and lived 22 years. Olympias, the 5-month-old

---

[97] Archias was one of the oligarchs at Thebes in 379 BC, and Lais was a beautiful woman. The reference is to the coup at the end of 379: supporters of democracy, disguised as courtesans, infiltrated a wild party and killed the oligarchs.

daughter he left behind, and Fortunesis her nurse, and Lauricia his wife erected this for a well-deserving husband with whom she lived 7 years. I inform you that everyone he conquered died. May the Manes who love him take care of him.

ILS 5121 = CIL 5.3466, tombstone at Verona. The advice with which this memorial closes is in the voice of Glaucus himself, not Aurelia.

Sacred to the memory of Glaucus, born in Modena, fought 7 times and died in the 8th, lived to be 23 years 5 days old. Aurelia and his friends erected this for a well-deserving husband. I advise you each to find your own guiding star; put no trust in Nemesis: I was deceived that way. Hail and farewell.

ILS 5152 = CIL 6.10172, at Rome

Eutychus Neronianus, freedman of Augustus, doctor at the morning *ludi*, erected this for himself and for Irene, freedwoman, dearest and most well-deserving wife, and for their children, free-born and freed.

ILS 5153 = CIL 6.10164, at Rome

Sacred to the memory of Cornelia Frontina, who lived 16 years 7 months. Marcus Ulpius Callistus, freedman of Augustus, her father, supervisor of arms for the great games, and Flavia Nice his most virtuous wife erected this for themselves and for their children, free-born and freed.

Charioteers, as well as gladiators, had families.

ILS 5281 = CIL 6.10063, at Rome

Sacred to the memory of Musclosus, driver for the Red faction, born a Tuscan, won 682 palms: 3 for the Whites, 5 for the Greens, 2 for the Blues, 672 for the Reds. Apuleia Verecunda his wife erected this in his memory.

ILS 5142 a-e. These graffiti from Pompeii indicate that the stereotype of women's attraction to gladiators can be found in popular culture as well as in literature. The fifth one is fragmentary.

a. He makes the girls sigh! Celadus the Thraex, 3 victories, 3 crowns.

b. The girls' glory! Celadus the Thraex

c. Celadus the girls' glory!

d. Thraex Celadus, *retiarius* Crescens, masters of the dolls

e. Crescens the *retiarius* and the girls at night ....

ILS 5282 = CIL 6.10062, at Rome. This is one of our few references to the short-lived new colors introduced by Domitian; see also the selection from Cassius Dio in chapter 3.

Sacred to the memory of Epaphroditus, driver for the Red faction. He won 178 times and as a freedman won 8 times for the Purple faction. Beia

Felicula erected this for a well-deserving husband.

Women with money might build public buildings just as wealthy men did.

ILS 5628 = CIL 10.5183, from Casinum in Latium

Ummidia Quadratilla, daughter of Gaius, built an amphitheater and a temple for the people of Casinum with her own money.

Chapter 6

Politics and Sports

These texts show various ways in which politics and sport interacted in Rome. *Duoviri*, aediles, and other magistrates put on *ludi* or *munera* as part of their official duties, paying for them largely from their own money. These games served as advertising for politicians hoping to advance to the next office. Laws for newly-incorporated colonies, like those for the Colony of Julia Genetiva excerpted here, specified exactly who was to put on *ludi* and what public funds they could use. Other laws controlled behavior at the spectacles, especially where different classes of people could sit and what they must wear. The higher classes got better seats, closer to the stage or the action; slaves would be relegated to the back. Such laws dated back at least to the *Lex Roscia*, proposed by Lucius Roscius Otho in 67 BC, and remained in force through the Empire, although some emperors were fussier than others about enforcing them. See also the description of Julius Caesar's delayed *munus* for his daughter, in chapter 1; ILS 5628, in chapter 5.

Inscriptions

Roman inscriptions testify to the importance of games and are part of the evidence connecting gladiator shows with funerals. Leading citizens would give *ludi* and *munera* or would build theaters, amphitheaters, and other public buildings.

ILS 5627 = CIL I,2, 1632 = ROL public works 55: in the amphitheater at Pompeii, from about 100-80 BC

Gaius Quinctius Valgus, son of Gaius, and Marcus Porcius son of Marcus, *duoviri* for the census year, to honor the colony, gave spectacles at their own expense to the colony and gave to the colonists a burial ground to be used in perpetuity.

ILS 5706 = CIL I,2, 1635 = ROL public works 59: at Pompeii, from about 90-80 BC

Gaius Ulius son of Gaius, and Publius Aninius son of Gaius, *duoviri* with judicial authority, arranged for the building of a Spartan-style sweating room and a room for massage, and for repairs to the portico and the palaestra, by decree of the colony's senators. They did this using the money that by law was to be spent on *ludi* or on a memorial. They ensured the work was acceptably completed.

CIL I,2, 1578 = ROL epitaphs 105: on a sepulcher at Carinola, from about 60 BC

Lucius Papius Pollo, son of Lucius, of the Teretine tribe, *duovir*, in honor of his father Lucius Papius, son of Lucius, of the Falernian tribe, gave honeyed wine and pastry to everyone residing in the colonies of Sinuessa and Caedex, and gave a gladiatorial *munus* and a meal to those in the colonies of Sinuessa and to the Papii. He set up a memorial costing 12,000 *sesterces* in accordance with his father's last will and testament and with the approval of Lucius Novercinius Pollo, son of Lucius, of the Pupinian tribe.

Cicero, *In Defense of Murena* 38-40, 67, 72

Lucius Murena was on trial for bribing the voters in the election for the consulate in 63 BC. Cicero, who was then consul himself, spoke for the defense. Lucius Roscius Otho had passed the *Lex Roscia* about seating in the theater just four years earlier, in 67. Note the reference to places in the forum: before permanent amphitheaters were constructed, *munera* and *venationes* would take place there.

38-40: But if you consider these things [Murena's military record] trivial which are really quite serious, and put urban support ahead of military, then at least do not scorn the elegance of his *ludi* and the magnificence of his theater: they were so useful to his campaign. Why do I say the people, the ignorant crowd, are so pleased with *ludi*? It's no great wonder. Although this is a sufficient reason: the voters are the people, the assembly of the common folk. Therefore if the magnificence of *ludi* is pleasing to the people, it's no wonder it was helpful to Lucius Murena. But if we, who are kept away from common pleasures by our work, and in this very work find many other pleasures, nevertheless enjoy the *ludi*, why do you marvel at the unlearned crowd? Lucius Roscius Otho, a brave man and a friend of mine, has restored to the Equestrian order not only its dignity but also its pleasure. His law relating to *ludi* is therefore very welcome to everyone, in that this most respectable order now again has both splendor and the enjoyment of amusement. Believe me, men do like *ludi*, even those who pretend otherwise—as I found out in my own election, for I too had a theatrical rival. If I, who gave three *ludi* as aedile, was nevertheless moved by Antony's *ludi*, do you, who as it happens gave none, think this silver theater that you mock is no rival to you?

67: You said the senate had decreed, on my motion, that if anyone had gone to see the candidates about bribery, if people they hired followed the candidates around, if they gave people places for gladiator shows by tribes, or if banquets had been given to the people, such things would be considered violations of the *Lex Calpurnia*.[98]

---

[98] The *Lex Calpurnia* (or *Lex Acilia*), passed in 67 BC, provided that anyone who bribed voters would be ineligible for election ever again. Bribes could include not just monetary payments to individuals but also tickets for shows, public banquets, or other gratifications to the electorate as a whole.

72: But spectacles were given by tribes and the people were invited to banquets. Even if this was done by Murena, jurors,—and it was not, it was done by his friends in the customary way—nonetheless, urged on by the fact itself, I recall, Servius, how many votes the discussion of these questions in the senate took away from us. For what time was there, in our memory or in the memory of our fathers, when this—call it currying favor or call it generosity—did not take place: when a man didn't give places in the circus and the forum to his friends and fellow-tribesmen?

Letters to friends 2.11, 8.4, 8.6, 8.8, 8.9

Marcus Caelius Rufus was a younger friend of Cicero's who was elected aedile in 50 BC. At this time Cicero was governor of Cilicia, in southern Asia Minor. Caelius wanted some exotic animals for the games he was to give as aedile, and in every letter he wrote to Cicero at this time, he closes with a paragraph about panthers.

June, 51 BC (8.4)
Caelius to Cicero

Once again I remind you about Sittius's bond (for I want you to know this matters a great deal to me); and similarly about the panthers, if you could acquire some from Cibyra and arrange for them to be sent to me. Besides this, (for I have heard as a fact that the king in Alexandria is dead), please tell me what you'd advise me to do, how that kingdom is getting on, and who's running it.

October, 51 BC (8.8)
Caelius to Cicero

Curio treats me well, and has put a burden on me by his generosity, for if he had not given me those panthers that he'd had shipped from Africa for his own *ludi*, I could have done without a *venatio*. But now, since I'm going to have to give one, could you please arrange for me to have some kind of beasts from where you are? I know I'm always asking this of you. I remind you about Sittius's bond. I'm sending my freedman Philonem and the Greek Diogenes, to whom I've given commissions and a letter for you. Please take care of them and the matter I've sent them about. I've explained in the letter they will give you just how much this matters to me.

autumn, 51 BC (8.9)
Caelius to Cicero

In just about every letter I've written to you about the panthers. Patiscus has sent Curio 10 panthers; you'll be put to shame if you don't send a great many more. Curio has given me those 10 and 10 more from Africa, so don't think that the only gifts he knows how to give are farms. If you remember to get some hunters from Cibyra and also send a letter to Pamphylia (where, they say, more can be found), you will do what you want. I'm quite worried about this now because I think I'm going to have to provide the whole *ludus* with no help from my colleague. Please, please, make yourself do this. You're always willing to take care of things, as I for the most part am not. In this business you don't have to do anything except talk, that is give the orders and directions. And as soon as the panthers are caught, you have people to feed them and ship them, the people I sent to deal with Sittius's bond. I think if you give me any hope in your next letter, I'll send more men to you.

February, 50 BC (8.6)
Caelius to Cicero
   P.S.: You'll be put to shame if I don't have Greek panthers.

April, 50 BC (2.11)
Cicero the General, greetings to Marcus Caelius the curule aedile
   Did you ever think it could happen that I would be at a loss for words, not only your fancy rhetoric but even our everyday speech? But it's true, I'm speechless, because I'm very worried about what will be decided about the provinces.[99] A great longing for the city has me in its grip. I miss my friends and family, and especially you. I am tired of the province, either because I seem to have acquired the kind of reputation that should not so much be sought as feared, or because there is no work to be done here worthy of those of us who can and have carried on the great work of the republic, or because the fear of a great war hangs over us, which I could escape if I left at the scheduled time.

   As for the panthers, those who are in the business of hunting them are diligently complying with my instructions. But there is an amazing shortage, and those panthers that we do have are complaining that there are no traps laid in my province except for them. Therefore the panthers state they have decided to depart from our province and take up residence in Caria. Nonetheless, it will be sedulously attended to, by Patiscus in particular. Whatever panthers there are will be for you, but I certainly do not know how many there will be. Your aedileship is very important to me, by Hercules; the very day reminds me, for today is the date of the Megalensian *ludi*. Please be very diligent about writing me everything about the state of the republic, and I shall consider reports most certain if they come from you.

Suetonius, *Life of Julius Caesar*, sec. 10
Julius Caesar, 100-44 BC, was aedile in 65.
   When Caesar was aedile, he gave *venationes* and *ludi* both with his colleague (the other aedile) and on his own. This way, he took credit

---

[99] Cicero is particularly concerned about whether his own term as provincial governor will be extended.

himself even for the expenses they shared. His colleague Marcus Bibulus made no secret of this, saying "The same thing has happened to me as to Pollux: the temple in the forum of the twin brothers is called the Temple of Castor, and similarly mine and Caesar's generosity is called Caesar's alone." Caesar even gave a gladiatorial *munus*, but with rather fewer pairs than he had intended, because the group he collected from everywhere was so large that his enemies were threatened, and got a law passed that no one could keep a large troupe of gladiators in Rome.

Inscriptions

ILS 6085, the *Lex Julia municipalis*, a law passed by Julius Caesar in 46 BC, during his dictatorship and before he went to Spain. The law is written on a bronze tablet found outside Rome. Two passages are relevant to sports.

77-79. Whenever someone produces *ludi* at Rome or within one mile of the city of Rome, nothing in this law will abridge his existing right to place and erect a stage, a platform, or whatever else is required for these *ludi*, in a public place, and to use this place on those days when the games are going on.

108-125. Whatever towns, colonies, districts, or places of assembly of Roman citizens there are or will be, no one in such town, colony, district, or place of assembly may be enrolled, now or in the future, as a senator or decurion, nor may he speak in debate or vote, who has been condemned for a theft he has committed, ... (a list of other disqualified persons follows), ... who has been a *lanista* or an actor, or who has been a procurer. Anyone who despite these regulations becomes a decurion or senator or speaks in debate in any town, colony, district, or place of assembly, will be fined 50,000 sesterces, and anyone who wishes may bring action against him to collect the fine.

ILS 6087, the *Lex Ursonensis*, or Laws of the Colony of Julia Genetiva. These were the original laws of this colony at Urso, founded under Julius Caesar's dictatorship. The laws were written around 44 BC, possibly after Caesar's death, but our copy, on four bronze tablets with some pieces missing, was made about a hundred years later. In addition to specifying what magistrates must put on *ludi*, the laws also set up rules for seating arrangements at *ludi*.

70. *Duoviri*, except for the first ones elected after passage of this law, must produce a *munus* or theatrical *ludi* during their magistracy, dedicated to Jupiter, Juno, Minerva, and the other gods and goddesses, on a date determined by the decuriones, four days long and lasting through the greater part of each day, to the extent possible. In those *ludi* or that *munus* each one must spend no less than 2,000 sesterces of his own money, and each *duovir* will be permitted to spend at most 2,000 sesterces of public money. They will be permitted to do so without penalty provided no one spends or assigns for this purpose any of the money which by this law

must be given or assigned to rites or sacrifices that take place in the colony or in any other public places.

71. Aediles in their magistracy must produce a *munus* or theatrical *ludi* to Jupiter, Juno, and Minerva, three days long and lasting the greater part of each day, to the extent possible, and one day in the circus or in the forum of Venus. In these *ludi* or that *munus* each one must spend no less than 2,000 sesterces of his own money and each aedile may spend 1,000 sesterces of public money. The *duoviri* or the prefect should have charge of giving and assigning this money and the aediles may take it without penalty.

125. Whatever place at the *ludi* is given, assigned, or left to the decuriones, from which place the decuriones may watch the *ludi*, no one may sit in that place unless he is at the time a decurion of the Colonia Genetiva; or he holds the power and authority of a magistrate by vote of the colonists or on orders from Gaius Caesar the dictator or a consul or proconsul; or he has equivalent power and authority in the Colonia Genetiva; or he has been given a place in the decuriones' place by a decree of the decuriones of the Colonia Genetiva, passed when no fewer than half the decuriones were present for debate. Nor may he bring anyone else into this place to sit, nor order anyone to sit there with intent to defraud. If anyone, contrary to this law, sits there with intent to defraud, or if anyone brings or orders anyone to sit there, contrary to this law and with intent to defraud, however often he behaves contrary to this law he shall be liable to pay a fine of 5,000 sesterces to the colonists and colony of Julia Genetiva, and anyone who wishes has the right and ability to prosecute or sue him before the *duoviri* or the prefect to recover the money.

126. A *duovir*, aedile, or praetor who puts on theatrical *ludi* for the Colony of Julia Genetiva, or anyone else who puts on theatrical *ludi* for the Colony of Julia Genetiva, must bring the Genetivan colonists, inhabitants, guests, and travelers to seats, and must give, distribute, and assign places, as the decuriones shall decree and decide, when no fewer than fifty decuriones are present for debate on this matter. Whatever shall be decided and decreed by the decuriones about the giving and assigning of places is to be lawful and valid by this law. He who puts on the *ludi* shall not bring people to seats otherwise or in another way, nor order them to be brought, nor give a place nor order it to be given, nor allot places nor order them to be allotted, nor assign places nor order them to be assigned, otherwise or in another way; and when a place is given, assigned, or allotted, they must sit there, nor shall he knowingly and with intent to defraud allow anyone to sit in any other place. Anyone who behaves contrary to this law, in each instance, as often as he behaves contrary to this law, shall be liable to pay a fine of 5,000 sesterces to the colonists and colony of Julia Genetiva, and anyone who wishes has the right and ability to prosecute or sue him before the *duoviri* or the prefect to recover the money.

127. Whenever anyone puts on theatrical *ludi* for the Colony of Julia Genetiva, no one may go into the orchestra to watch the *ludi* except a magistrate of the Roman people or one who serves in place of a magistrate, one with juridical authority, or any senator of the Roman people who is or will be present, or any son of a senator of the Roman people who is or will be present, or any prefect of engineers attached to a magistrate of the province of Farther Spain, or those who by this law are or will be permitted to sit in the decuriones' place. Nor may anyone bring anyone to a seat there or permit anyone to sit there, as he shall wish it to be done rightly without intent to defraud.

128. Whoever will be a *duovir*, aedile, or prefect of the Colony of Julia Genetiva, he shall carry out his magistracy in each year to the best of his ability, without intent to defraud; shall attend to sanctuaries, temples, and shrines as the decuriones shall determine; shall take care of circus *ludi*, sacrifices, and public banquets in whatever way the decuriones shall decree about these matters: creating magistrates, putting on circus *ludi*, procuring sacrifices, making banquets. And concerning the aforementioned matters, whatever the decuriones decide and decree shall be legal and valid, and all those to whom this law pertains, whatever they are required to do by this law, they shall do so without intent to defraud. If anyone behaves contrary to this law, as often as he behaves contrary to this law he shall be liable to pay a fine of 10,000 sesterces to the colonists and colony of Julia Genetiva and anyone who wishes has the right and ability to prosecute or sue him before the *duoviri* or the prefect to recover the money.

ILS 5052 = CIL 11.3613: at Caere, from AD 25.

... Augustus..., Gaius Cercenius freedman of Gaius, Lucius Magilius freedman of Lucius, ..., Titus Mercello, Lucius Tuccius Celsus the messenger of the consuls and praetors, Lucius Arruntius Helenus freedman of Lucius, Gaius Titinius freedman of Gaius and deputy, ... [6 other fragmentary names of freedmen] put on Latin and Greek *ludi* 24 February through 1 March and gave crustula and mulsum[100] to the people. In the consulate of Marcus Asinius Agrippa Cossus and Cornelius Lentulus.

Augustus, *Res Gestae* ("Accomplishments") 22-23

Augustus was the first real "emperor" in Rome. He lived from 63 BC to AD 14, and his reign, once it got started, was a time of general peace and prosperity. This selection comes from Augustus's own record of his accomplishments.

Three times I gave gladiatorial *munera* in my own name and five times in the names of my sons and grandsons, and about 10,000 men fought in these *munera*. Twice I summoned athletes from everywhere to give a spectacle to the people in my own name, and a third time in the name of my grandson.

---

[100] Crustula are cookies or small cakes, and mulsum is a kind of honey cake.

I gave *ludi* in my own name four times, and on behalf of other magistrates 23 times. On behalf of the College of Fifteen, with Marcus Agrippa as my colleague, in the year when Gaius Furnius and Gaius Silanus were consuls, I gave the *ludi saeculares*. In my 13th consulate, I was the first to give the *ludi* dedicated to Mars, which since that time the consuls have given every year, according to law. I gave the people *venationes* with African beasts 26 times, in my own name or those of my sons or grandsons, in the forum or in the amphitheater, and in these about 3,500 animals were killed.

[Sec. 23] I gave the people a naval battle as a spectacle, across the Tiber in the place where the grove of the Caesars is now. The excavation for the lake was 1,800 feet long and 1,200 feet wide. In this battle 30 ships fought, more or less, triremes and biremes with prows equipped for ramming. Aside from the rowers there were about 1,300 men on these ships.

Suetonius, *Life of Augustus*, sec. 43-45

Here Suetonius talks about Augustus's games in general, not any specific occasion. As evidence, he quotes from the passage of the *Res Gestae* excerpted above. Augustus's various laws about seating and behavior at the spectacles are part of his concern for morality in Roman life.

In the variety and frequency of his spectacles Augustus excelled everyone. He said "I gave games in my own name 4 times, and on behalf of other magistrates who were away or were not able to give them, 23 times." He gave several theatrical *ludi* in different parts of the city, featuring actors in all languages. He put on spectacles not only in the forum or the amphitheater but also in the circus and in the Saepta, sometimes consisting of nothing but a *venatio*. He also gave athletic games at the wooden bleachers he made in the Campus Martius. He staged a naval battle, for which he excavated an area near the Tiber, where the Grove of the Caesars is now. On these days he stationed guards in the city so that, with most people at the games, idlers and vagrants would not cause trouble. In the circus, he brought out chariot drivers, racers, and beast-killers, some of them young men from the best families. He also put on the Trojan game very frequently, with older and younger boys, since he believed that this exhibition showed off the natural qualities of the Roman people and their ancient and noble custom. When Nonius Asprenatis was injured by a fall in the Trojan game, Augustus gave him a golden torque and allowed him and his family to bear the cognomen Torquatus. But before long Augustus stopped putting on the Trojan game, when the orator Asinius Pollo complained, nastily and enviously, that his nephew Aeserninius had fallen and broken his leg.

Roman knights would sometimes perform in theatrical and gladiatorial shows, at least before the senate forbade it. After that, almost no one of good family made an exhibition of himself, (except the young Lucius Icius, but then he was less than two feet tall, weighed 17 pounds, and had an immense voice). One day when there was a *munus*, Augustus brought Parthian hostages, who had just been released, through the middle of the arena to the spectacle and seated them behind him in the second row. He used to put unusual and noteworthy items on public view, even on days without spectacles, for example a rhinoceros on the Saepta, a tiger in the theater, or a snake 50 cubits long in the assembly area.

Once he was giving a circus spectacle to fulfill a vow, but he fell sick, so he led in the images of the gods while reclining in his litter. Then, too, when he was dedicating the theater of Marcellus with *ludi*, the joints of his curule chair came loose and he fell on his back. And at his grandsons' *munus*, when the people were afraid the building was going to fall and he could not reassure them, he got out of his own place and sat in the part that they were most nervous about.

[Sec. 44] Augustus made rules and organized the seating arrangements, which had been very confused and quite lax, prompted by the disrespect shown to a senator, who was unable to get a seat at a very crowded *ludus* at Puteolus. A law was passed as a result that whenever public spectacles were given, the first row of seats should be reserved for senators. Ambassadors of Rome and its allies were forbidden to sit in the orchestra, since he found out that some of them were giving their places to freedmen. He seated soldiers separately from the people. He assigned specific places for married plebeians, gave the boys their own section with their *paedagogi* next to them, and ruled under penalty of religious sanction that no one in mourning could sit in the middle rows. He would not permit women to watch even the gladiators, which had formerly been permitted at the annual ritual *ludi*, except from the highest rows. The only exception was the Vestal Virgins: he gave them their own place in the theater, by themselves, across from the praetor's raised seat. He kept the entire female sex so far away from the sight of athletes that when he gave *ludi* for his elevation to pontifex, he put off a pair of boxers to the next morning, and said that he did not want women to come to the theater that day before the fifth hour.

[Sec. 45] Augustus himself used to watch circus spectacles from his friends' and freedmen's upstairs rooms, but sometimes from the bench in the circus where the gods' statues were, and sitting with his wife and children. He would go away from the spectacle for several hours or even several days, asking pardon of those who would have the responsibility of presiding in his absence. He was indeed present often enough, and doing nothing else, partly to avoid the kind of reputation his father [Julius] Caesar had had—the people disapproved of the way Julius used to spend his time writing letters and reading books during the spectacle—and partly because he enjoyed watching them, something he never tried to hide and even often said was appropriate for a free man. He would frequently give crowns and large prizes out of his own pocket even at other people's *munera* and *ludi*. In every Greek game he watched, he always honored the contestants according to their merits. He was especially happy to watch boxers, especially Latins, and not only those who made a regular practice of fighting, whom he would even match with the Greeks, but also troops from small towns, who would fight boldly in a tight spot, though without good technique. In short, he felt that everything to do with offering a public spectacle was worthy of his attention. He preserved and increased the privileges of athletes; forbade gladiator shows to the death, without *missio*; and took away the magistrates' old right to punish actors, except at the *ludi* and the theater (under the old law, they could do so at any time or place). Nonetheless, he always regulated the athletic contests and the gladiatorial fights most strictly.

Inscription

ILS 5639 = CIL 13.1642, at Feurs, France.

Consecrated to the deified Augustus. For the well-being of Tiberius Claudius Caesar Augustus Germanicus.[101] Tiberius Claudius Capito, son of Aruca, priest of Augustus, rebuilt in stone at his own expense the theater which Lupus son of Anthus had built in wood.

Tacitus, *Annals* 14.17

The incident described here took place in AD 59, while Nero was emperor. Nuceria (modern Nocera) was east of Pompeii. Although Roman sports did not involve teams representing or playing for their cities, as modern teams do, any public gathering might be an excuse for displays of civic pride or rivalry.

Around the same time, a trivial incident gave rise to serious carnage between the Nucerians and the Pompeians, at a gladiator spectacle that Livineius Rebulus was putting on. (He had been expelled from the Senate, as I have explained elsewhere.)[102] It started with playful taunts between the two towns. Soon they were hurling insults—then rocks, and finally they took up swords. The Pompeians won the fight; the show was taking place in their town. So, many of the Nucerians were carried to Rome, heavily wounded, and many people mourned the deaths of children or parents. The emperor allowed the Senate to pass judgement on this incident. The Senate asked the consuls, who referred the matter back to the Senate. The result was that the Pompeians were forbidden to hold such public assemblies for the next ten years, and certain clubs that they had organized illegally were disbanded. Livineius and the other instigators of the riot were punished with exile.

---

[101] This is Claudius, emperor from AD 41-54.
[102] This explanation is presumably in one of the lost parts of the *Annals*.

Tacitus, *Annals* 14.20-21

Suetonius also mentions these games in his biography of Nero; see selection in chapter 5.

When Nero was consul for the fourth time, and Cornelius Cossus was the other consul [AD 60], he instituted an entertainment at Rome in the style of a Greek contest, to be held every four years; there was much discussion about this innovation, as there is about almost everything new. In fact, there were those who had said even Pompey should have been censured for building a permanent theater. Before his time, the *ludi* were held with hastily constructed banks of seats and a stage built for the occasion. In even earlier times, the spectators used to stand, since it was felt that if they sat down together in a theater, they would pass whole days in idleness. People now said that the old spectacles should be preserved, such as the praetors would give, and without forcing any citizen to compete. They felt ancestral customs were slowly being abolished, from the bottom up, by imported licentiousness, and as a result every kind of corruption could be found in the city. Youth was degenerating from study abroad, from training in gymnasia, and from constant leisure and immoral loves. The emperor and the senate approved this: they not only permitted the free exercise of vice but even forced Roman noblemen to be defiled by performing speeches and songs on the stage. So what was left except that they strip completely naked, put on boxing thongs, and practice with their fists instead of military weapons? Would justice be increased and the jury-panels of knights perfected in the performance of their important duty if they listened skillfully to wrong notes and sweet voices? The nights, too, were given over to shame, so that there was no time left for decency, but in the disorderly crowd all the most immoral people could dare to have in the dark whatever he coveted by day.

[Sec. 21] This licentiousness did please most people, but they called it by a nicer name. There were many who did not despise the attractions of the spectacles as they were at the time, actors brought in from Etruria, race-horses from Thurii. Once we took possession of the provinces of Greece and Asia, we took more trouble over *ludi*, but no Roman of good family stooped so low as to be a professional actor in the 200 years from the triumph of Lucius Mummius [146 BC] at which that kind of spectacle was first offered to the city. Still, it was a thrifty idea to build a permanent theater instead of constructing one every year, at great expense, only to be torn down. Similarly, since the magistrates would run out of money if they also had to give Greek contests, which the people were asking for, they would be given to the republic at the emperor's expense. Victories for orators and poets would be an incentive to their talents, and no judge would consider it a serious crime to share in the honest, permissible pleasures of music. A few nights of happiness rather than wantonness would be given to everyone, nights of bright light in which nothing illicit could be concealed. Certainly the spectacle took place with no significant blemish, though the plebeians were not even a little excited, because although some plays were given, mimes and pantomimes were forbidden since this was a sacred competition. No one took first prize for eloquence, but Caesar was announced as victor. Everyone wore Greek clothes for several days, and then the fashion died out.

Inscriptions

ILS 5053 = CIL 10.1074: at Pompeii, from the first century AD. This monument, presumably a sepulcher, lists five members of the family.

1. Clodia, daughter of Appius, public priestess of Ceres by a decree of the decuriones.

2. Lassia, daughter of Marcus, public priestess of Ceres by a decree of the decuriones.

3. Appius Claudius, son of Marcus, of the Palatine tribe, clerk, magistrate of the district of blessed Augustus.

4. Appius Claudius Menenius Flaccus, son of Appius. *Duovir* for administering the laws for three terms at four-year intervals, appointed military tribune by the people. In his first duoviral term he held *ludi* for Apollo in the forum, with a procession, bulls, *taurocentas*, assistants, three pairs of *pontarii*, troops of boxers in both Latin and Greek styles, all kinds of theatrical spectacles, and pantomimes with Pylades.[103] He also gave 10,000 *sesterces* to the public treasury on behalf of the *duoviri*. In his second duoviral term he held *ludi* for Apollo in the forum, with procession, bulls, *taurarios*, assistants, and troops of boxers. The next day by himself he held a spectacle with 30 pairs of athletes, 5 pairs of gladiators, 35 additional pairs of gladiators, and a *venatio* with bulls, *taurocentas*, boars, and bears. He gave another *venatio* with various animals together with his colleague. In his third duoviral term he gave *ludi* in the first faction and additional theatrical entertainment with his colleague.

5. Lucius Gellius Menenius Calvus, son of Lucius, decurion of Pompeii.

Clodia daughter of Appius built this monument at her own expense for herself and her family.

ILS 5143 = CIL 4.1179, at Pompeii. Gnaeus Alleius Nigidius Maius is named in a number of inscriptions from Pompeii, allowing us to reconstruct not only his own career, but also the structure of the town's government. Several of the inscriptions are announcements for games given by Maius.

Gnaeus Alleius Nigidius Maius the quinquennalis[104] will exhibit 30 pairs of gladiators and *suppositicii* at Pompeii on 24-26 November, and

---

[103] "Pylades" became a title for any star pantomime actor, after the name of the first tragic pantomime actor during the time of Augustus.

[104] A quinquennalis is a local town official who is elected every 5 years to a 1-year term.

there will be a *venatio* for Maius the fortunate quinquennalis.

ILS 5144 = CIL 4.1177, at Pompeii, on the wall of the baths. Fragmentary.

At the dedication ... the *munus* of Gnaeus Alleius Nigidius Maius ... there will be a *venatio*, athletics, *sparsiones*, and awnings.

ILS 5653 = CIL 10.855, 856, 857. On the podium of the amphitheater at Pompeii. These inscriptions indicate who controlled tickets for each section or "wedge" of seats.

a. Marcus Cantrius Marcellus, son of Marcus, *duovir* for *ludi* and lights, in charge of making up three wedges by decree of the decuriones.

b. Numerius Istacidius Cilix, son of Numerius, *duovir* for *ludi* and lights.

c. Lucius Saginius, *duovir* for *ludi* and lights with juridical authority, this wedge by decree of the decuriones.

d. Lucius Saginius, *duovir* for *ludi* and lights, this wedge by decree of the decuriones.

e. Master of the suburban district of blessed Augustus, for the *ludi*, by decree of the decuriones.

Suetonius, *Life of Domitian*, sec. 4

Domitian became emperor after his brother Titus, in 81; he was the younger brother, born in 51. Suetonius was alive, adult, and active during his reign, so was an eyewitness to some of the things he describes.

Domitian frequently gave magnificent, sumptuous spectacles, not only in the amphitheater but also in the circus, where in addition to the annual races for two- and four-horse chariots he put on a double battle, with both cavalry and foot soldiers. In the amphitheater he put on a naval battle. He even put on *venationes* and gladiator shows at night, with lamps, and there were not only men but also women fighters. Besides the quaestors' *munera*, which he had re-instituted after an interval in which they did not take place, it was always important to him that he gave the people the power of choosing two pairs from his *ludus* whom he would bring in dressed up as if they were the newest members of the imperial court. At every gladiatorial show a little boy with a prodigiously small head would stand in front of his feet, dressed in scarlet. He used to talk to the boy frequently, sometimes in earnest. The following was certainly overheard: Domitian asked him whether he knew any reason why he shouldn't make Maecius Rufus prefect of Egypt in the next cycle of promotions. Domitian gave naval battles with almost as many ships as the regular fleet. He dug out and walled in a lake next to the Tiber and watched the naval battles even during major rainstorms.

He also put on the *ludi saeculares*, figuring the date not from the most recent ones under Claudius but from those that Augustus had given. In these games, on the day for the circus, so that it would be possible to have 100 races, he reduced each one from seven laps to five.

He also set up a competition to be held every four years for Capitoline Jupiter, with three parts (musical, equestrian, and gymnastic), and with rather more events than there are now at the crown games. There were contests in Greek and Latin prose orations. In addition to singers accompanying themselves on the cithara, there were events for cithara with chorus and for cithara alone without singing. There was even a foot-race for maiden girls. Domitian presided over the contests wearing sandals and a purple robe in the Greek style, with a golden crown on his head decorated with images of Jupiter, Juno, and Minerva. The priests of Jupiter and of the Flavian Family sat next to him, similarly dressed except that on their crowns there was also an image of Domitian himself. Every year in Alba he celebrated the *Quinquatria* of Minerva, for which he instituted a committee of magistrates from whom some would be chosen by lot each year to run the festival and be responsible for putting on outstanding *venationes* and theatrical shows as well as a competition for orators and poets.

Domitian three times gave a dole to the people of 300 *sesterces* each, and between the events of a *munus* would hold an immense banquet. At the Feast of the Seven Hills, when bread baskets are given to the senate and the knights and little baskets of food to the plebs, he was the first one to start eating. The next day he scattered all kinds of things from the *missilia*, and because most of them fell among the ordinary people, he announced that tokens should be thrown 50 at a time into the sections where the knights and senators were sitting.

Martial

Several of Martial's poems talk about seating arrangements in the theater. Under Domitian the old rules were once again being enforced, leaving the first fourteen rows only for the knights. The old dress code was back again, too. Leitus and Oceanus, not otherwise known, are theater attendants whose job was to enforce these rules.

4.2

Horatius, alone in the crowd, was watching a *munus* in a black cloak, while the plebs and the lower class and the highest along with their sanctified leader all sat in white. Suddenly snow started to fall from the sky—now Horatius watches in a white cloak.

5.8

Our Lord and Master made a rule by which seating arrangements would be settled, and the front row would receive only the Equestrian

Order. Phasis praises it in the theater, ruddy in a purple cloak, dropping these pompous pearls of wisdom: "At last we can sit in comfort. Now dignity is restored to the knights; we will not be pressed or besmirched by the crowd." While he's idly saying this sort of thing, Leitus orders him to take off his haughty purple.

5.14

Nanneis was always accustomed to sit in the front row. When the spectators were let in, he was rousted 2 or 3 times around the auditorium and finally sat down behind Gaius and Lucius, right between their seats. There the ugly fellow looked out of the hood over his head, looking at the *ludus* with one eye. From here the poor fellow gets thrown out and goes into the aisle, half propped up at the end of a bench and badly received. He spreads his knees: one sits with the knights and one stands for Leitus.

5.23

You'd been dressed up in green, Bassus, back when the laws were silent about seating in the theater. But when a kind and painstaking censor revived the old rules, and the knights heard the Ocean was the right thing, now all your best clothes are dyed with scarlet and purple-fish, and you think you'll get a good reputation that way. The Four Hundred[105] don't have cloaks, Bassus, otherwise my Cordus would have one before any of the knights.

5.25

"Chaerestratus, you don't have the Four Hundred, so get up, here comes Leitus. Stand up, go, run, hide." Hey, I'm gone; will anybody call me back? Is there any friend who'll spread his wealth around? Whom have I written about, made famous so everybody talks about him? Who doesn't want to visit the Styx? I ask you, isn't this better than smearing the stands with a red cloud and dying them through and through with saffron yellow? Better than giving the 400 to a horse that will sense it, so Scorpius's golden nose can shine everywhere? O uselessly rich man, deceiver of your friends, do you read this and applaud? Then may your fame perish!

5.27

I admit, you have the talent, the energy, the manners, and the breeding of a knight—but everything else is plebeian. The fourteen rows are not for the likes of you; you must sit in white and look at the ocean.

6.9

Laevinus, you sleep in the Pompeian Theater—do you complain if Oceanus wakes you up?

---

[105] This refers to the property qualification for being a knight: knights were those who had an income of 400,000 sesterces a year.

Juvenal, *Satire* 3, 152-159, 171-179

Juvenal's third satire is about the problems of city life; these sections indicate why even festivals are better in the country.

152-159: Unfortunate Poverty has within herself nothing harsher than that she makes men ridiculous. "He should go out, if he has any shame, and get off the equestrian cushion, since his property is not up to the legal minimum. Let the pimps' boys sit there, born in some brothel; let the auctioneer's elegant son applaud with the cultivated scions of crest-snatchers[106] and *lanistae*. That was how foolish Otho[107] wanted it when he divided us up."

171-179: There's a large part of Italy, if the truth be told, where no one puts on a toga until he's dead. Even when the grassy theater cultivates the dignity of festival days, and the familiar comedy returns at last to the stage, and the little country boy trembles in his mother's lap at the gaping mouth of the pale masks, even then you will see the orchestra and the stands dressed just alike. White tunics suffice for even the chief aediles as the garment of distinction.

Satire 10, 72-81, 356

This is the satire imitated by Samuel Johnson's "The Vanity of Human Wishes" in 1749.

72-81: What about Remus's plebeian crowd? It follows fortune, as always, and hates those fortune condemns. If fortune had favored Sejanus, if Tiberius had been crushed in his old age, that same populace would be calling Sejanus "Augustus" right now. For a long time now, since we've been buying their votes for nothing, they've stopped caring. The Roman people which once dispensed power, consulships, legions, everything, now sits on its hands and anxiously waits for just two things: bread and circuses.

356: All you should pray for is a sound mind in a sound body.

Pliny the Younger, *Letters* 10.31 and 32

As an imperial legate in the province of, Bithynia, Pliny got involved with the punishment of criminals in the province.

Gaius Plinius to the Emperor Trajan

Saving your greatness, lord, it is appropriate that you lower yourself to my concerns, since you have given me the right of referring things to you about which I am in doubt. In many states, especially Nicomedia and Nicaea, certain people who have been condemned to hard labor, to the

---

[106] Crest-snatchers are probably gladiators, especially those who fight against *murmillones* and Samnites, both of whom had devices on their helmets.

[107] Lucius Roscius Otho, the proposer of the *Lex Roscia*.

ludus, or to similar punishments are carrying out the duties and functions of public slaves and even receive an annual stipend in this capacity. When I heard this, I was greatly at a loss and considered for a long time what I ought to do. I felt it would be too strict to send them back to their punishment after such a long time, since many of them were by now old men and, by all accounts, were living honest and moderate lives. On the other hand, to keep condemned men in public positions did not seem to me entirely proper. Moreover, I considered that if they were not working, it would be useless for the state to support them, and dangerous if it did not. I have of necessity left the entire matter undecided until I could consult you. Perhaps you will ask how it came about that they were released from the punishments to which they were condemned: I too asked that question, but received no answer I could give to you. Although the decrees by which they were condemned have been published, no published record permits their release. There are those, however, who say these men were released by the intercession of the proconsuls or legates. This is plausible; certainly no one would have dared release them without authority.

Trajan to Pliny

We will remind you that you were sent into that province because so many things there were manifestly in need of improvement. And this will particularly require correction: that those condemned to punishment were not only released without authority, as you write, but even brought back into trusted official positions. Those among them, therefore, who were condemned in the last ten years and were not released by a suitable authority should be returned to their punishment. If older cases are found, old men condemned more than ten years ago, let us assign them to those offices which are not far from punishment: attending the baths, cleaning the sewers, paving the roads.

Letters 39 and 40

Pliny also had to supervise public works, many of which were for sports and spectacles.

Gaius Plinius to the Emperor Trajan

The theater at Nicaea, lord, is largely built, but is not finished, and I hear (I have not been able to flush out the actual plans) that it has sucked up more than ten million sesterces—which I fear have been wasted. Huge, gaping cracks have opened up as the structure has settled, either because the ground is wet and soft or because the stone is light and friable. The question now is whether it should be completed, abandoned, or even pulled down. The supports and the bases by which it has been propped up over and over seem to be not so much solid as sumptuous. Many private citizens still owe what they have pledged for the theater, for example the colonnade around the auditorium and the gallery above, but all these things are being deferred due to delays in work that must be completed first. These same Nicaeans have begun to restore a gymnasium that was destroyed by fire before I came, making it much bigger than it had been, and they have already spent a certain amount on that; there is a risk that it will be useless, since it is a disorderly and messy business. The architect, moreover, although he is jealous of the fellow who began the work, say the walls cannot support the weight of the building, even though they are 22 feet thick, because their centers are filled with rough stone and they are not clad in brick.

The Claudiopolitans, too, are putting up a huge bathhouse in a low-lying spot with a mountain looming over it, digging it out rather than building it up. They are even using the money which the councilors, inspired by your generosity, either offered for your ceremonial entrance or are collecting at our insistence. So, since I fear that because of public spending there your *munus* here, which is worth more than any money, may come off badly, I am driven to request that you send an architect, not only for the theater but for this bathhouse too, to figure out whether, given what has been spent so far, it is more useful somehow to finish what has been started or to correct what must be corrected and put off what can be put off, so that we do not spend badly on additions in hopes of preserving what we've already spent.

Trajan to Pliny

What is to be done about the theater that stands unfinished in Nicaea you will best determine and decide yourself. It is enough if you tell me the decision you have come to. Be sure to demand the additional works from the private citizens once the theater they were promised for is complete.

The Greeklings are very fond of gymnasia; perhaps therefore the Nicaeans went into the construction of this one with high spirits, but they will have to be content with one that will be adequate.

You can decide how to advise the Claudiopolitans about the bathhouse they've begun to build in an unsuitable spot. You cannot lack for architects. There is no province that does not contain skilled and clever people. Do not assume it is faster to send one from Rome, since even here they generally come from Greece.

Fronto, *Elements of History* 17

This selection comes from the fragmentary *Elements of History*. Trajan was emperor from 98-117, and Lucius Verus was co-emperor with Marcus Aurelius (his brother) from 161-169.

Both Trajan and Lucius are blamed for sending for actors from Rome to come to Syria. But just as we see the highest trees the most violently shaken by the winds, so it is the greatest virtues that envy is most ready to slander. Whether Trajan is to be considered more excellent in war or in peace I leave undecided, but even Spartacus and Viriathus were competent at arms. In the art of peace, however, hardly anyone stands before Trajan in the eyes of the people, if anyone has even equaled him. Is it not this popularity that inflames Trajan's detractors? It appears to come from a deep knowledge of the art of governing. The emperor was not careless even about actors or other people concerned with the stage, the circus, or the arena, since he knew there are two things that especially grip the Roman people: the price of grain and the spectacles.[108] A government recommends itself by what it does in trivial matters no less than in grave ones: to neglect the serious ones brings larger punishment, but to neglect the lesser brings greater ill will. The food-dole provokes less acrimony than the spectacles, since the dole only placates certain specific individuals while the spectacles are for everyone.

Inscriptions

ILS 5648 = CIL 8.7988, at Philippeville, France, AD 225

Marcus Fabius Fronto, augur, prefect with judicial authority, gave theatrical *ludi* and in addition 1,000 *denarii* to build a theater in the name of his son Senecio. Promised in the second consulate of Fuscus and the consulate of Dexter, on the fifth of January, and dedicated under the same consuls on 31 March.

ILS 5077 = CIL 8.7960, at Philippeville, France

To the Spirit of the Colony of Veneria Rusicadis; consecrated to Augustus. Marcus Aemilius Ballator, praetor, gave 10,000 sesterces in his own name to the people at their request to erect and maintain a theater, and in addition set up two statues at his own expense, of the Spirit of our fatherland and of Annona protector of the city. At their dedication he gave *ludi* with *missilia*. Space provided by decree of the decuriones.

ILS 5661 = CIL 8.9065, at Aumale in Mauretania, AD 227.

Decennius Claudius Juvenalis Sardicus completed the turning-posts and eggs[109] as well as the judges' platform, in memory of members of the Claudian family: Rufinianus his son, a youth of good reputation; Rufinianus and Victorinus his grandsons; Longania Primosa, a woman of good reputation, his wife and the mother and grandmother of Claudians; and Kaninia Respecta, a woman of good reputation, his sister-in-law and mother of Claudians, in the year of the province 188.

ILS 5074 = CIL 8.895, 8S.12425: in Zaghuun, Algeria, from AD 239. From this

---

[108] Compare the selection from Juvenal, *Satire 10*, above.
[109] "Eggs" were lap-counters for the races.

inscription and a few others, we deduce that in this province aediles usually gave a *missilia* instead of *ludi* as they did at Rome.

To Mars Augustus, protector of our lord the emperor Caesar Marcus Antonius Gordianus Pius Felix Augustus, pontifex maximus, awarded tribunal power twice, consul, father of his country. Quintus Calvius Rufinus, aedile, at his own expense and that of his colleague Titus Aelius Annus Litorus, upon being honored as an aedile gave money to the common treasury in place of a *missilia*. Calvinus Rufinus, aedile, dedicated this statue and gave a spectacle of boxers and athletes at his own expense. Space provided by decree of the decuriones.

ILS 5633 = CIL 6.1763, 6.32089, at Rome. The emperors' names tell us this inscription was written between AD 425 and AD 450; it refers to repairs to the Flavian Amphitheater.

Good health to our lords Theodosius and Placidus Valentinianus Augusti! Rufius Caecina Felix Lampadius, distinguished man, urban prefect, replaced the sand in the amphitheater as well as the podium and rear posts, and also repaired the risers for seats.

ILS 5635 = CIL 6.1716b, 6.32094b, at Rome. This inscription dates from about AD 508 and shows that the Flavian Amphitheater was still in active use at the very end of the Roman empire.

Decius Marius Venantius Basilius, distinguished man, urban prefect, patrician, ordinary consul,[110] at his own expense restored the arena and podium, knocked to ruins in a dreadful earthquake.

ILS 5075 = CIL 8S.14783: somewhere in North Africa, date unknown.

To Gaius Egnatius Paperia Felix son of Gaius, a most blameless aedile, for service to a friend. At the dedication [of this statue] Egnatius declared a day sacred to the Liberaliores instead of the gymnastic exhibition and *missilia* that aediles usually give. He gave the spectacle at his own expense to the entire community and in addition gave theatrical *ludi* and a banquet to the people. Space provided by decree of the decuriones.

ILS 5651 = CIL 10.1217, Avella Vecchia

To Numerius Plaetorius Onirus, priest of Augustus, honored with the privileges of a decurion, by public subscription among the Avellans, because he increased the grain endowment at his own expense and in his own name by 10,000 sesterces, and because he gave awnings to the theater with all necessary equipment at his own expense. Space provided by decree of the decuriones.

---

[110] An "ordinary" consul is one elected to office at the start of the year, as opposed to a "suffect" consul who would take over halfway through the term. In the Republic, suffect consuls were only rarely required, for example if an ordinary consul died in office. During the Empire, it became customary for the ordinary consuls to resign halfway through their year of office, so that each year four men could be consuls (and thereafter have the privileges of ex-consuls).

Chapter 7

Attitudes about Sport and Spectacles

Selections in this section give some idea what various Romans thought about *ludi* and *munera*. Here we see explicit discussion of the place of sport in Roman society. The questions Cicero, Seneca, Tertullian, Pliny, and Augustine raise are still relevant to the modern world: is popular culture a waste of time for an intelligent person? Are people harmed by watching violent entertainment? Does society spend too much money on sports?

Every writer represented here is an educated, wealthy man. The lower classes of the Roman empire did not leave us letters or poems, but we can get some idea of their views, and of some women's views, from the graffiti and tombstones presented in other chapters. Of course it is an oversimplification to say that "all intellectuals" or "all of the upper classes" disliked sports: selections in earlier chapters, especially those from Suetonius, Ovid, and Martial, show educated, wealthy men and women—even emperors—enjoying chariot races, *munera*, and the theater. It is also an oversimplification to say that the rise of Christianity destroyed Roman sports, though the Christian writers Tertullian and Augustine certainly make their disapproval clear. In the end, Roman gladiator combats and chariot races continued almost to the very end of the Empire, despite the boredom and disgust of some of the upper classes.

See also the selections from Tertullian in chapter 1.

Cicero, Letters to friends 7.1

This letter refers to *ludi* given by Pompey the Great in August of 55 BC. Pompey had built the first stone theater in Rome and these *ludi* were for its dedication. Marius and Cicero had adjoining villas in the country, at Pompeii.

Marcus Cicero to Marcus Marius, greetings.

If some bodily sickness or infirmity kept you from coming to the *ludi*, I would say you were lucky rather than wise. But if you felt these things everyone else marvels at should be an object of contempt, and had not wanted to come even if you had been healthy, I would have rejoiced at both the health of your body and that of your mind, seeing you paying no attention to what other people marvel at for no reason, and benefiting from your leisure. Indeed you could certainly have enjoyed yourself, left almost alone in this pleasant place. I have no doubt that you spent those mornings reading in that bedroom of yours from which you have such a good view of the bay of Stabiae. Meanwhile those who had left you there were half asleep in the crowded theater, watching the mimes. As for the rest of the days, you must have spent them in pleasures arranged by your own judgment. We, on the other hand, had to put up with Spurius Maecius's choice of plays.

If you want to know, they were nicely prepared *ludi*, but not to your taste, if it's anything like my own. First, to honor Pompey, came onto the stage those actors who I would have thought should stay away for their own honor. Your old heart-throb, my friend Aesopus, was in such bad shape that everyone said he should leave the stage. When he began to take the oath [in the play], his voice failed him at the part "if I knowingly deceive." What else can I tell you? You know what the rest of the plays were, and they didn't even have the charm that mediocre plays sometimes do. The over-spectacular production took all the fun out of it, and I don't doubt you're just as glad to have missed it. What's the pleasure in 600 mules in *Clytemnestra*, or 3,000 wine bowls in the *Trojan Horse*, or different kinds of arms for foot-soldiers and cavalry in some battle? Although this stuff won popular admiration, it wouldn't have given you any pleasure.

If on those days you gave your Protogenus work to do, provided he was reading you something other than my orations, then you had at least as much pleasure as any one of us. I don't think you like the Greek or Oscan *ludi*,[111] especially since you can see Oscans in your own senate, and as for Greeks, you dislike them so much you won't even take the Greek road to get to your villa. And how can I think you missed the athletes, since you hate gladiators? Pompey himself acknowledged they were a waste of money and of oil. There were *venationes*, twice a day for five days; magnificent, no one denies that; but what possible pleasure can there be for a civilized man in watching some weak man shredded by a very strong beast, or a strikingly beautiful animal run through by a hunting spear? And if you've seen one *venatio*, you've seen them all; we who saw this one certainly saw nothing new.

The final day belonged to the elephants. The common crowd had great admiration for them and no pleasure at what they saw. No, indeed; they pitied the elephants, and felt that there was a kind of community between those beasts and the human race.

So you don't get the idea that I'm not only happy but utterly free, on the days of the theatrical *ludi* I also nearly killed myself on the trial of your friend Caninius Gallus. If I had such a friendly audience as Aesopus had, by Hercules I'd cheerfully give up this business and live with you and people like us.

---

[111] The reference to "Greek and Oscan *ludi*" means plays given in those languages. Oscan, an old Italian language related to Latin, was the language of the Atellan farce.

Pliny the Elder, *Natural History* 35.51

Paintings, mosaics, and sculptures of gladiators were popular throughout the Roman empire; compare the fictional Trimalchio's decorations in the selections from Petronius in chapter 2.

One of Nero's freedmen, when he was giving a gladiator *munus* at Antium, filled up the public porticos with a completely lifelike picture of gladiators and all the attendants. Many generations have considered this the best kind of picture. But the idea of painting gladiator *munera* for display in public places came from Gaius Terentius Lucanus. He gave 30 pairs in the forum over three days for his grandfather, who had adopted him, and put a painting of the event in the temple of Diana.

Seneca

The following selections come from the "moral letters," small philosophical discourses addressed to Seneca's friends.

Letter 7, sec. 1-5

You ask what you should especially avoid. The crowd. You cannot yet trust yourself to be safe in a crowd. I'll admit a weakness of my own: I never bring back the same morals as I brought out. Something of my inner composure is disturbed and something of what I have escaped comes back. What happens to sick men, who after long weakness cannot be taken anywhere without further harm, also happens to us, whose hearts are recovering from a long disease.

[Sec. 2] Being with a lot of people is harmful. There is no one who will not recommend some vice to us, or press it upon us, or smear us with vice without our knowledge. And the more people we are with, the greater the danger.

And nothing is so damaging to good morals as to hang around at some spectacle. There, through pleasure, vices sneak in more easily.

[Sec. 3] What do you think I'm saying? I come back more greedy, more desirous of honor, more dissolute, even more unfeeling and cruel, because I have been among people. By chance I happened to be at the spectacle at noontime, expecting some witty entertainment and relaxation, to rest men's eyes from the gore. It was the opposite. Whatever fighting there was before was comparative mercy. Now there was pure murder, no more fooling around. They have nothing to shield them, and with the whole body exposed to the blow, no one ever misses.

[Sec. 4] Many people prefer this to the ordinary pairs and the fighters people ask for. Why wouldn't they? No helmet or shield pushes the sword away. Where is the defense? Where is the skill? These things are just to delay death. In the morning men are thrown to lions and bears; at noontime, to the audience. They order those who have killed matched with those who are going to, and they keep the winner around for another bout. The fighting ends in death, and it happens by fire and the sword. They do this while the arena is empty.

[Sec. 5] "But he was a thief, he killed somebody." So? Because he killed, he deserves to suffer the same; why are you so wretched as to deserve to watch? "Kill him! Hit him! Burn him! Why is he scared to face the sword? Why does he fall over like a coward? Why doesn't he die like a free man? Let him be whipped in his wounds. They should get matching blows on their naked chests." When there's a break in the spectacle: "Cut some throats meanwhile, so it's not completely quiet."

Letter 70, sec. 19-23, 26

Here Seneca holds up gladiators and bestiarii as examples of bravery. See also the selection from Plutarch in chapter 5.

Do not think that only a great man has the firmness to break out of the slavery of the human condition. Do not judge that this can only be done by a Cato,[112] who finished off with his bare hands what he could not do with his sword. Men of the most worthless class have escaped to safety by great inspiration, and if they were not permitted to choose the time or means of their own death, they snatched up whatever was at hand, making weapons by brute force of what was not naturally harmful.

[Sec. 20] Not long ago in a school for bestiarii there was a German who was being trained for the morning spectacles. He went aside to relieve himself; there was no other place he could be alone without a guard. There he took the wooden stick with a sponge attached, used for what is most unclean. He stuffed the whole thing down his throat, closed his mouth, and gave up his spirit. This was an insult to death. It was not a pretty or proper way to die; what is stupider than to die daintily?

[Sec. 21] What a strong and worthy man, who should have been allowed to choose his own fate. How bravely he would have used a sword, how spiritedly he would have leapt into the farthest depths of the sea or from a precipitous cliff. Though he was completely destitute, he found the ways and means of his own death; from this you should know that nothing needs to delay death except willpower. Let everyone judge this man's case on its merits, provided he agree that the vilest death is to be preferred to the most elegant slavery.

[Sec. 22] Because I began with the example of a base man, I will continue. For everyone will expect more of himself if he sees that even the most contemptible can hold death in contempt. We think men like Cato, Scipio, and the others we usually hear of with admiration are too high for us to

---

[112] Cato Uticensis, 95-46 BC, was the "Stoic saint," always scrupulously fair (if a bit strict), who killed himself rather than live under Julius Caesar.

imitate, but I shall show that there are as many examples of such virtue in a school of *bestiarii* as among the leaders of a civil war.

[Sec. 23] Recently, as the prisoners were being taken in a cart to the morning spectacle, one of them nodded as if falling asleep. He put his head down so far that he could put it between the spokes of the wheel, and held himself in this position until he broke his neck in the turning of the wheel. He escaped in the same cart that was taking him to be punished.

[Sec. 26] I promised you more examples from the same *munus*. In the second part of a naval battle, one of the barbarians took the spear he was to use on his opponents and plunged the whole thing into his own throat. "Why, why didn't I escape from all this torment and derision a long time ago?" he said. "Why do I wait for death while I am armed?" This spectacle was so much more beautiful, in which men learned how much more honorable it is to die than to kill.

Juvenal, *Satire* 11, 193-204

This satire contrasts the simple pleasures of someone who lives like an old-fashioned Roman with the luxury of the modern world.

Meanwhile, they're holding the Megalensian spectacle for the Phrygian Mother and dropping the annual *mappa*. The praetor sits there as if celebrating a triumph, but he's the horses' prey. And, if I may say so without offending the immense, uncountable plebs, today all Rome is in the circus. The noise hurts my ears, from which I infer the Greens have won. And if they had lost, you would have seen this city sad and stunned, just like when Hannibal beat the whole army and killed both the consuls. Let the young men watch; it's OK for them to have wild noise and betting, and to sit next to their favorite girls. We'll skip dressing up and let our wrinkled old skin drink up the spring sunshine.

Pliny the Younger, *Letter* 9.6

This letter can be compared with the one from Cicero to Marius, above.

Gaius Plinius to his friend Calvisius, greetings.

I've passed all this time quietly and most happily among my books and notes. "How could you do that in the city?" you ask. The circus was going on, a type of spectacle I'm hardly interested in at all. Nothing new, nothing unusual, nothing one needs to see more than once. I'm always amazed that so many thousands of men so childishly love to watch the horses run and the men standing in the chariots. If they were attracted to the speed of the horses or the technique of the charioteers, there'd be some reason for it, but they cheer for a bit of cloth, they love their flag. If right in the middle of the race two drivers switched colors, the favor of the crowd would switch too. Suddenly they'd be screaming out the names of those drivers and those horses that they ignored before. So much charm and so much authority in a filthy tunic: I can understand this from the ordinary folks, whose own tunics are filthier, but even certain serious men feel this way. When I think about people like that, who so insatiably long for something empty, cold, and impermanent, I take a certain pleasure in never having been taken by this pleasure. So I spend these days freely writing letters, while others waste them on perfectly useless activities. Farewell.

Letter 9.23

Not all intellectuals disliked or avoided the circus.

Gaius Plinius to his friend Maximus, greetings.

It has often happened to me, as I'm prosecuting a case, that all 100 of the judges, who normally restrain themselves during a trial, maintaining their authority and seriousness, would suddenly be driven to stand up and praise me; and often I have hoped to gain a certain significant fame among the senate; but nothing has ever made me happier than this story I just heard from Cornelius Tacitus. He said there was a Roman knight sitting with him at the last circus. After a certain amount of learned conversation the knight asked, "Are you from Italy or the provinces?" Tacitus answered, "You know me, at least from your reading." To which the other said, "Are you Tacitus or Pliny?" I cannot express how delightful it is to me that our names would be used as if they belonged to the books, and that each of us is known by readers if not by sight.

Tertullian, *On Spectacles*

Sec. 18: on Greek-style games. This selection comes from the same book of Tertullian's as the discussions of the origins of various games in chapter 1.

But if you assert that the stadium is mentioned in the Scriptures,[113] you will be right. But you will not deny that what goes on in the stadium is not worthy to be seen: punches, kicks, blows, all the wantonness of the hands, and any kind of injury to the human face, which is the image and likeness of God. You will never approve of worthless running and throwing and even more worthless jumping. Strength which is harmful or useless will never please you, and neither will body-building that goes beyond God's creation. You will hate seeing men fattened up for the leisure of the Greeks. And wrestling is the work of the devil: he was the first to strike at men. He has the moves of a snake, he is tenacious at holding on, good at twisting and binding up, but fluid at slipping away. You have no need for a crown; why go hunting for pleasure from crowns?

---

[113] St. Paul uses many athletic metaphors in his letters.

Inscription

ILS 5163 = CIL 2.6278, from Andalusia. This text, inscribed on a bronze tablet, records a speech given in the Senate in response to a proposal by the emperor Marcus Aurelius and his son Commodus, who were joint emperors from AD 176 —180. The senator refers to the emperors' proposal as their "divine speech." The beginning and the end of the senator's proposal are missing. The emperors' proposal was to put an end to the substantial tax on revenues from gladiator *munera*, and this senator further proposes that the cost of gladiators should be regulated and reduced. He hopes to reduce the burden on certain priests, whose offices required them to put on expensive *munera*.

[1] Such a plague cannot be cured by any medicine. Indeed, our Princes, whose only desire is to revive and restore public health, now overwhelmed and worn out by such a great disease, have first turned their attention to finding out what gives the disease its strength, where these foul and illicit revenues get their rights, who instituted and fosters the use, as if it were legitimate, of what is prohibited by all human and divine laws.

[5] The public treasury was repeatedly invoked. The public treasury was invited, not for its own sake but as a pretext for other people's butchery, to have a third or fourth share in the filthy plunder. So they have taken the public treasury entirely out of the arena. After all, why should Marcus Aurelius and Lucius Commodus provide for the treasury with the arena? All of these princes' money is pure, neither stained with human blood nor defiled by profits from filthy sources; it is supplied as scrupulously as it is spent. So this money would go away, whether it is twenty or thirty million sesterces a year; you are adequately providing for the state by your own frugality. Why not even cancel part of the 5,000,000 sesterces in debt owed by the *lanistae*? What have they done to deserve this, I ask you? They do not deserve it, say the Emperors, but it will be a small consolation for preventing them from their accustomed robberies, and henceforward they are invited to serve humankind on our terms.

[12] O great Emperors, who know the only certain cure must take into account the interests even of bad people who have made themselves essential! Your foresight is now bearing fruit. Your speech was only lately read to us, but when the rumor spread that the profits of the *lanistae* were being curtailed and the public treasury had given up all that tainted money, at once the priests from the most faithful lands of Gaul began running around and rejoicing together.

[16] There was one man who bemoaned his bad luck at being made a priest and had decided to appeal to the Princes. But now he is asking his friends, "Why did I need to appeal? the most holy Emperors have removed the entire burden that oppressed my property. Now I *want* to be a priest, and I embrace the responsibility of *munera* which I formerly detested." Thus not only he but many others had requested the favor of

an appeal. Now this sort of case has a different form: people are appealing when they are *not* made priests. What other opinion can there be, therefore, about such a great and advantageous plan as yours, than the opinion that I believe each and every one of us holds, rejoicing in his innermost heart?

[23] I therefore advise that we first give thanks to our greatest Emperors, who, by wholesome remedies and with no regard for the claims of the public treasury, have restored the threatened stability of our cities and saved the fortunes of the leading men from impending ruin; and all the more magnificently, since, although no one would have blamed them if they retained those things they had instituted to be nurtured and that were confirmed by long usage, nevertheless they most fairly judged it was entirely inappropriate to their plan to conserve what had been badly instituted or to institute what would be badly conserved.

[27] Although some may believe that we should express one concise opinion on everything our greatest Princes have brought before us, I shall nevertheless, if you approve, speak about individual points in particular, using the very words of the most holy speech, brought into the light of judgment, so that there will be no opportunity for distorted interpretations.

[29] I therefore advise that the *munera* called *assiforana* should retain their form but should not exceed expenses of 30,000 sesterces. For those giving *munera* of 30,000 to 60,000 sesterces, gladiators should be supplied in three equal groups: the highest price in the first group should be 5,000 sesterces, in the second 4,000, in the third 3,000. From 60,000 to 100,000 sesterces the gladiators should be divided in three groups: in the first rank the highest price should be 8,000 sesterces, in the second 6,000, then 5,000. Then from 100,000 to 150,000 sesterces there should be five groups, of which the price in the first is 12,000 sesterces, in the second 10,000, in the third 7,000, in the fourth 6,000, and last 5,000. Further, from 150,000 to 200,000 sesterces and whatever is spent above and beyond that, the price of the lowest gladiator should be 6,000 sesterces, above him 7,000, the third 9,000, the fourth 12,000, and then up to 15,000. And this should be a settled amount for the best, attractive gladiator.

[35] Further, in all *munera* distinguished by classes, the *lanista* must furnish half the total number out of the ordinary group or "flock."[114] The better members of the flock may fight as a group at 2,000 sesterces each, and no one from the flock will go for less than 1,000 sesterces.

[37] Since the *lanistae*, hoping to increase profits, may say they cannot supply an adequate number from the flock, they must know they will be

---

[114] Gladiators of the "ordinary group" or the "flock" may be inexperienced or less competent fighters, or those who have not yet become well known. They were presumably less interesting to the spectators, but cheaper.

required to transfer as many as required from those they consider better, to make up the required number for the flock. Thus on any given day the entire *familia* will be divided into equal parts, and on any given day at least half of them will be in the flock.

[40] To see that the *lanistae* carry this out as diligently as possible will be the responsibility of those who preside over the provinces, and the legates, quaestors, legionary legates, distinguished men with juridical authority, or procurators of our greatest Princes, as the provincial governor orders, and also of those procurators who preside over provinces. But in the Transpadane and throughout Italy this responsibility will be given to the prefects of the grain supply, if they are present, or the curator of roads, or if he is not present either, to anyone with juridical authority or at last to the prefect of the fleet.

[45] I advise further the following rule concerning the proceeds: that each gladiator make an individual bargain for the money received for his fighting, and that a free man should receive one quarter, a slave one fifth. Concerning the prices of gladiators I have already advised the recommendations of the divine speech be followed, but that these prices should apply to those cities that suffered from relatively high prices for gladiators. If the Republic is weaker in certain of its cities, they should not observe the same rules that are written for the stronger cities, nor should they be burdened beyond their strength. The highest, median, and lowest prices in public and private dealings should be ascertained by whoever presides in the province, since these are provincial cities, by a magistrate with juridical authority, the curator of the province, the prefect of the praetorian fleet, or the procurator of our greatest Princes, depending on which holds the major magistracy in the city.

[51] These dealings should be inspected at the end of ten years and examples of *munera* given in each city should be considered; when this has been done, the three prices may be retained or the man whose task it is may decide to determine a new threefold price scheme to be used thereafter. The proconsuls who have recently set out should be informed that each must complete this task within his own year; those who by lot are not governing provinces, within a year.

[56] But as for the *trinqui*[115] which the cities of the most splendid Gauls look forward to according to the ancient and sacred ritual, the Gauls need offer no more to a *lanista* than 2,000 sesterces, for as the greatest Princes proclaimed in their speech, a procurator need not supply criminals condemned to the arena for more than 6 gold pieces.

[59] The priests of the provinces who will have nothing to do with *lanistae* will accept gladiators hired by previous priests, or free men on their own authority, but after the *munus* they will pass them on to their

---

[115] The *trinqui* were apparently a particular festival held in Gaul.

successors at cost, and they will not sell anyone for a greater price than would have been due to a *lanista*.

[62] Anyone who comes before the tribune of the plebs and declares his intention to fight as a gladiator will have in accordance with this law a price of 2,000 sesterces. If after he is freed he returns to fighting, his value may not exceed 12,000 sesterces.

Augustine, *Confessions* 6.8

In this selection, Alypius is a young friend of Augustine's from the same town.

Alypius left the country enchanted for him by his parents and set out for Rome to study law. There he was, incredibly, seized by an incredible desire for the gladiatorial spectacle. Here's how it happened. He loathed and detested such things, but some of his friends and fellow students, who ran into him after lunch one day, brought him to the amphitheater to see the cruel and deadly *ludi*. Alypius protested vehemently and resisted their efforts, saying, "Even if you drag my body into that place and sit me down, how can you get me to pay attention to the spectacles, or even to look at them? I'll be there in body only, and I will conquer you and these spectacles of yours." His friends were then all the more determined to get him inside, perhaps wanting to find out if he could do it. When they got in and found seats, the whole place was hot with monstrous passion. Alypius closed his eyes, shut the door to his mind, and forbade himself to get involved with such evils. But it would have been better if he could have closed his ears, too! For at one moment, when something happened in the fight and he was struck by a huge shout from the whole audience almost like a physical blow, his curiosity got the better of him. He had almost prepared himself to see what it was, and whatever it was to disdain it and conquer it, but when he opened his eyes he was wounded as gravely in his soul as the other man was in his body—the gladiator he had lusted to see. And Alypius was more wretchedly defeated than the man whose death had given rise to the shouting. When he saw the blood, he drank in the monstrosity and did not turn away, but kept his eyes glued to the sight and was steeped in the madness, unaware of what was happening. He was fulfilled by the evil of the contest and drunk on the cruel pleasure. And he was no longer the same person who had come, but just one of the crowd he had come to, a true member of the gang who had brought him there. What more is there to say? He watched, he shouted, he got feverishly excited, and he took away with him a madness by which he was goaded to come back, not only with those friends who had first dragged him in, but on his own and even bringing others along.

Glossary

aedile: a Roman official in charge of markets, traffic, and the streets. Being elected aedile was a stepping-stone to greater offices. Aediles were generally expected to put on games.

amphitheater: the place where gladiatorial fights are held. It is a round or oval building, with seats on all sides and a floor of sand in the center. *Venationes* are also held here, and some amphitheaters could be flooded for naval battles.

Apuleius: Apuleius lived in the second century AD in Rome and in Africa. He was a philosopher and teacher, but also wrote a novel, the *Golden Ass* or *Metamorphoses*, about a young man, Lucius by name, who gets turned into an ass.

arena: the sandy floor of the amphitheater, from *harena*, which is the Latin word for sand

Artists of Dionysus: the guild or professional association of actors in Hellenistic Greece and in the Roman empire

assiforana: *munera*, generally given by a private citizen, for which admission is charged

athletic: in a Roman contest, refers to "Greek-style" games with events drawn from the programs of the major Greek games (the Olympian, Pythian, Isthmian, and Nemean games). Athletic events included boxing, wrestling, and foot races.

auctoratus (pl. *auctorati*): Roman citizen who chooses to sign on as a gladiator

Augustine: Saint Augustine, Bishop of Hippo in North Africa, lived from 354 to 430, toward the end of the classical period at Rome and the beginning of Late Antiquity. He wrote various theological works, but his most popular book is his *Confessions*, a spiritual autobiography written around AD 400. It is in straightforward, very readable Latin.

Augustus: Augustus, born Gaius Octavius in 63 BC, was the first Roman emperor (although Suetonius begins his "Twelve Caesars" from Augustus's adopted father Julius). As a monument to his career, he wrote up his accomplishments and had them posted in various places in the empire, in either Latin or Greek depending on what the local population could read. This text, called *Res Gestae* or *Accomplishments*, was written in the last year of Augustus's life; he died in AD 14. Most subsequent emperors took "Augustus" as a title or cognomen, so most references to "Augustus," like references to "Caesar," in later texts refer to whoever is emperor at the time.

balteus: belt to hold a sword

bestiarius (pl. *bestiarii*): a person who fights against wild animals in the arena. *Bestiarii* were not gladiators, and were considered lower than gladiators.

Cassius Dio: Dio wrote a history of Rome, in Greek, at the beginning of the third century AD. He was consul in AD 205 and again in 229.

censor: a Roman official in charge of maintaining the lists of citizens by classes. During the Republic, two censors were chosen every five years to serve for a year and a half. During this time they listed all the citizens according to their wealth, classifying them as senators, knights, ordinary citizens, or freedmen. Senators who had committed crimes or offended against public morals could be removed from the senate. By the time of Augustus, however, the office ceased to be important.

Cicero: Marcus Tullius Cicero was a politician and statesman in late Republican Rome; he was born in 106 BC and assassinated in 43. His surviving writings include speeches, philosophy, a little poetry, and a great many letters to friends, colleagues, and family. The collected letters also include some of the letters Cicero received.

circus: the place where chariot races are held. As a building, it looks much like an amphitheater, with the race track in the center. In Rome, the Circus is usually the Circus Maximus. "Circus" in a Roman context never refers to what we would call a "circus."

cognomen: Roman citizen men generally bore three names, called praenomen, nomen, and cognomen in that order. For example, Marcus Tullius Cicero has "Cicero" as his cognomen. The nomen is the family name. The cognomen was originally an epithet or nickname given to some member of the family, then used by his descendants. It might describe or poke fun at some physical characteristic or it might refer to some accomplishment. A particularly distinguished Roman might acquire more than one cognomen. Slaves had only one name, and the custom was for a freedman to adopt his former master's praenomen and nomen and use his slave name as a cognomen. For example, when Cicero's secretary Tiro was freed, he became Marcus Tullius Tiro.

conditor: stable-keeper or overseer of the stables for a chariot-racing *familia*

consul: the highest-ranking magistrate in Rome. Two consuls were elected every year. During the Republic, they were the leaders of the state. During the Empire, they were less effective but just as prestigious; the emperor himself or his intended heir would often be one of the consuls. A year is most often identified by the names of the consuls who served; then, for example, Suetonius tells us Augustus was born "in the consulate of Marcus Tullius Cicero and Gaius Antonius."

contraretiarius: a gladiator who fights against a *retiarius*

cryptarius: the member of a *lanista*'s *familia* who is in charge of the "crypt" or building in which the gladiators train

curule chair: the special kind of chair, of a particular shape and generally inlaid with ivory, to which high-ranking magistrates were entitled. Curule magistrates are those who may use curule chairs: consuls, praetors, and curule aediles.

decurion (pl. **decuriones**): member of the town "senate" in a town or colony other than Rome

denarius (pl. *denarii*): unit of money, equal to four sesterces and comparable to the Greek drachma

duovir (pl. *duoviri*): member of a committee of two, typically the two senior magistrates of a colony

eiselastic: having to do with a triumphal entry. Eiselastic competitions were those whose victors were allowed to have a procession when they returned to their home cities, in just the same way as a victorious general would have a procession. This kind of procession is called a "triumph" and its major feature is that the general (or athlete) rides in a chariot drawn by white horses. The word "eiselastic" is from Greek words meaning "drive in."

Ennius: (239-169 BC) the first Roman poet to write an epic in the meter and style of Homer. He chose for his subject the history of Rome from its founding down to the present, and called the work *Annals*. It survives only in fragments.

essedarius: a gladiator armed like the driver of a British war-chariot

faction: The teams or "colors" in the circus are usually called "factions." There were four, the Red, White, Blue, and Green, during most of the Empire. Domitian introduced Purple and Gold factions, but this innovation did not last. At some point, the White faction merged with the Blue for administrative purposes, and the Red with the Green, though drivers continued to race under all four colors.

familia: the base meaning is "household." Referring to gladiators, a *familia* is the group, troupe, or school of gladiators belonging to a particular *lanista*. Referring to chariots, a *familia* is the group of drivers and horses belonging to a given stable; a *familia* would be associated with one of the four factions.

flamen (pl. *flamines*): a priest devoted to a particular god. There were originally three major *flamines*, devoted to Jupiter, Mars, and Quirinus (a god who watched over the Romans as citizens, rather than as soldiers, and sometimes identified with Romulus). There were also twelve minor *flamines*, and later *flamines* were created to superintend worship of deified emperors.

Floralia: an annual festival, starting on the 28th of April and going on for a week, sacred to Flora, the goddess of spring and flowers. The celebration included various combat sports, including gladiatorial fights, between prostitutes.

Fronto: Marcus Cornelius Fronto, 100-166, was an orator and teacher of rhetoric. His best-known pupil was Marcus Aurelius, who was emperor from 161-180. The *Elements of History* (or "Preface to History") was intended as the introduction to a history of Rome's wars against the Parthians. Fronto never did write the history, and the preface is fragmentary.

gallus: type of gladiator, otherwise unknown

Gellius: Aulus Gellius, who lived roughly from AD 130 to 180, wrote a collection of anecdotes called the *Attic Nights* for the instruction and amusement of his children.

gladiator: a fighter in the arena, usually a slave. The name comes from *gladius*, which means "sword." Most gladiators used swords, though some were armed with nets (the *retiarii*) or other weapons. Gladiators were classified according to the weapons they used; types of gladiator included the *essedarius*, the *gallus*, the *hoplomachus*, the *murmillo*, the *retiarius*, the *contraretiarius*, the *provocator*, the *sagittarius*, the *scissor*, the Samnite, the Thraex, and probably others. A group of gladiators, called a *familia*, was owned and managed by a *lanista*.

hoplomachus: heavily-armed gladiator; the name is from Greek words meaning "armed fighter"

Horace: The poet Quintus Horatius Flaccus (65-8 BC) was a contemporary of Augustus and a friend of Virgil. He wrote "satires," not as angry in tone as those of Juvenal, shorter lyric poems usually called the "odes," and longer discursive poems called "epistles," or letters in verse.

imperator: originally, any military commander, especially one who has won a major victory. Later, certainly in the second century AD and perhaps starting as early as Augustus, "imperator" became a title for the emperor.

inscriptions: texts written on stone monuments, gravestones, bronze tablets, or other objects. Inscriptions are important because they are (usually) contemporary with the events they describe, not works of history written later in hindsight. The texts include laws, dedications, epitaphs, and memoirs like the *Res Gestae* of the emperor Augustus.

instauration: Roman rituals had to be perfect. If there was any flaw in the performance of the ritual, it had to be done again. Flaws could include someone mispronouncing a critical prayer, or being unable to kill a sacrificial animal cleanly. The repetition of the ritual is called an instauration. Because *ludi* were religious rituals, they were subject to the rule of perfection. This meant the crowd could get a repeat performance of a play, for example, by convincing the presiding magistrate that the ritual was flawed and an instauration was necessary.

Juvenal: Decimus Junius Juvenalis lived from 55-127, which makes him contemporary with Pliny, Tacitus, and Suetonius. He wrote 16 poems called "satires" which attack various features of contemporary life, some quite angrily.

knight: Roman society was divided into classes based on wealth and political office. Senators were at the top; they were wealthy men who had held high elected office. Knights were next: those who had property worth 400,000 sesterces but were not senators. Originally, knights were the cavalry of the Roman army, but by the end of the Republic they were simply the wealthy businessmen.

lanista (pl. *lanistae*): someone who owns, trains, and manages a troupe or *familia* of gladiators

lex (pl. *leges*): law. Roman laws were generally referred to by the nomen of the magistrate who proposed them. For example, while he was consul, Cicero proposed a law increasing the penalties for briberies in elections; it is called the *lex Tullia* after him. The important law of 67 BC governing seating arrangements at public spectacles is the *lex Roscia*, from Lucius Roscius Otho, who proposed it.

Livy: Titus Livius (roughly 59 BC - AD 17) was a historian who lived in the reign of Augustus. He wrote a history of Rome from its quasi-legendary origins down to his own day. Only 35 of its 142 books survive, though we have summaries of the others.

Lucilius: This poet is considered the father of Roman satire, a poetic genre that Horace and Juvenal also used. He was born somewhere between 180 and 148 BC and lived to be an old man.

ludus (pl. *ludi*): public spectacles, including games and theatre performances; also a school, including gladiator schools. The base meaning of the word is play, game, jest, or joke. *Ludi scaenici* are theatrical *ludi*; *ludi circenses* are circus *ludi*, that is, chariot races.

ludi saeculares: "Hundred-year games," a festival that was supposed to be held every hundred years. A *saeculum* is a period of 100 years, or an age or era (sometimes also a generation). These are sometimes called the "secular games" but the meaning of "secular" in English has evolved so that this is misleading: the *ludi saeculares*, like all Roman *ludi*, were definitely a religious observance.

lustrum (pl. *lustra*): the ritual purification performed every five years by the censors. Connected with this ceremony was the census, which at Rome meant not only counting how many citizens there were but also determining officially which classes they belonged to (senators, knights, ordinary citizens, freedmen).

manica (pl. *manicae*): a sleeve, especially a sleeve made of chain mail to protect the sword arm. A *manicarius* was someone who made and maintained *manicae*.

mappa (pl. *mappae*): a napkin, in particular the one dropped by the presiding magistrate to start a chariot race in the circus

Martial: Marcus Valerius Martialis was active as a poet during the reign of the emperor Titus, and the *Book of Spectacles* commemorates Titus's completion and dedication of the Colosseum or Flavian Amphitheater, begun by his father Vespasian. Martial himself lived from about 40 to 104, and wrote fourteen additional books of epigrams, totaling some 1,500 poems.

Megalensia: an annual festival for Cybele, held on the 4th of April. The aediles were in charge of providing the *ludi* at this festival, the *Ludi Megalenses*.

mime: Roman theater included tragedy, comedy, mime, and pantomime. Tragedy and comedy were approximately what they were for the Greeks and what they are today. Mime was a less serious form, including singing and dancing, and performers in mime often did not wear masks as they did in tragedy and comedy.

missilia: a mechanism for distributing presents among the spectators at a *ludus*, by throwing them into the seats. The presents might be coins, fruit, small cakes, or the like, but were more often tokens to be turned in for food or other valuables. The mechanism was apparently a cloth basket, like a hammock, suspended from pulleys which could be moved along guide-ropes around the amphitheater.

missio: literally a sending away; permission given to gladiators to stop a fight before either one has been killed

morator: member of a chariot-racing familia who holds and steadies the horses as they are being loaded into the starting-gate.

munus (pl. *munera*): duty, office; public office; funeral honors and last rites for the dead; gladiatorial show

murmillo (pl. *murmillones*, also spelled *mirmillo*): a type of gladiator who had a fish as the crest on his helmet. *Murmillones* generally fought against *retiarii*.

obsonia: a pension or allowance, especially given to victorious athletes. Originally "obsonia" is the plural of "obsonium," meaning food or the food market; it is a loan-word in Latin from Greek.

Ovid: Publius Ovidius Naso lived from 43 BC to AD 17. Although he wrote a mythological epic, *Metamorphoses*, collecting various stories in which someone is turned into something, his most characteristic works are the various poems about love. The *Amores* are short poems about relationships, and the *Art of Love* is a fairly long "textbook" poem about how to conduct a love affair. Ovid also started a calendar in verse, the *Fasti*, but only finished the chapters for January through June.

paedagogus (pl. *paedagogi*): slave who watches the children and escorts them to and from school

paganus: The base meaning is an inhabitant of a district called a *pagus*, but the word comes to mean a country-dweller or a rural person. In a list of members of a *familia* or other group of gladiators, it may mean a "civilian," someone who is not a gladiator.

palus (pl. *pali*): pale or stake, especially one set up as a wooden dummy to practice sword strokes on

pantomime: form of drama, usually telling a story from myth. The main actor danced but did not speak or sing. He would usually play all the roles himself, though there might be a speaking actor on stage as well. Music was provided by instrumentalists and a chorus of singers.

Parasites of Apollo: Several inscriptions about actors refer to this group, an association of actors that included mime and pantomime performers as well as actors in "straight" plays.

Petronius: Petronius was probably a contemporary of Nero in the first century AD, though we do not know his exact dates or even his full name. His *Satyricon* is a novel of which only a part survives. In the part we have, a rich freedman called Trimalchio gives a dinner party.

Plautus: The comic playwright Titus Maccius Plautus lived at the very beginning of the second century BC; we don't know the dates of his birth or death, but most of his plays were produced between 200 and 184. His plays are boisterous farces, written in verse.

plebs: non-noble citizens, as opposed to the senators; a member of the plebs is a plebeian.

Pliny the Elder: Gaius Plinius Secundus (AD 23-79) is known to us as Pliny the Elder because he was the uncle of the other Pliny. He was a scientist who died investigating the eruption of Mount Vesuvius at first hand.

Pliny the Younger: Gaius Plinius Caecilius Secundus, or Pliny the Younger, lived from 61-112, so he had almost exactly the same lifespan as his friend Tacitus, and was a little older than his friend Suetonius. Pliny lived a fairly typical life for a Roman of the senatorial class, including holding some political offices. He saved and published a collection of his letters, which give a good picture of Roman life at the beginning of the second century AD.

Plutarch: Plutarch was a Greek who lived in the first century AD, from about 50 until after 120. He wrote in Greek about both Greek and Roman topics, including biographies of famous men.

pompa: a Greek word meaning a procession. The race "from the pompa" was the first race of the day, right after the procession that opened the *ludi*. These were special, perhaps because the horses were nervous or perhaps because the major race of the day was scheduled first (instead of last as at a modern racetrack).

praetor: a Roman official, higher than an aedile but lower than a consul. Their functions were at first military and diplomatic, later judiciary.

provocator: type of gladiator

Propertius: Sextus Propertius was born around 50 BC and died by 2 BC. He was therefore a younger contemporary of Virgil and Horace, and was a friend of Ovid's. He wrote lyric poems, many about love, in the same form as Ovid's love poems.

quadriga (pl. *quadrigae*): four-horse chariot, the usual kind for races in the circus. There were also two-horse chariots, called *bigae*, and chariots of six or more horses were occasionally used.

quaestor: the lowest-ranking major office in Rome, generally the first elected office an ambitious man would hold. Quaestors in Rome were responsible for the state treasury; others served as treasurers and paymasters accompanying consuls and praetors on military campaigns.

quindecemviri: board of 15, specifically the 15 men in charge of *ludi saeculares*

Quinquatria: an annual festival of Minerva. The Greater Quinquatria were on the 19th of March and the Lesser on the 13th of June.

Quirites: the Roman people in their capacity as citizens. The name probably comes from Quirinus, a very old god, identified with Romulus. The Romans could be called "children of Mars" when they were considered as soldiers, but were the Quirites or "children of Quirinus/Romulus" when they were behaving as citizens.

retiarius (pl. *retiarii*): a lightly-armored gladiator with a net and a trident, who often fought against *murmillones*

rudis (pl. *rudes*): a wooden sword, used for practice. A gladiator who had completed his service was presented with a *rudis*, so "to get one's *rudis*" meant to be discharged from gladiatorial service, to be allowed to retire.

Saepta: the enclosed place where Roman assemblies voted

sagittarius: gladiator who fights with bow and arrows; *sagitta* means "arrow" in Latin.

Samnite: gladiator armed like a warrior from Samnium, with sword and shield. They would wear a *balteus*, a *manica* on the sword arm (the right), and a small greave only on the left leg.

Saturnalia: a festival held each year on the 17th of December, honoring Saturn. At this festival Romans gave each other presents, and slaves were "free" for the day. Saturn was the father of Jupiter, who had to conquer him to become king of the gods; Jupiter threw Saturn into prison in chains. This story is adapted from the Greek story of Zeus and his father Kronos, but in Roman versions Saturn is not necessarily killed.

scissor: type of gladiator, known only from one inscription

secutor: type of gladiator, possibly one who chases others

Seneca: Lucius Annaeus Seneca (the Younger) wrote several tragedies but was primarily a philosopher. He was tutor to the young Nero and continued to be one of his advisors after he became emperor. He wrote several "moral letters," small philosophical discourses addressed to his friends. He was born at the end of the first century BC and died in AD 65.

sestertius (pl. **sesterces**): the basic Roman unit of money, often abbreviated HS. In the time of Augustus (early 1st c. AD), an unskilled laborer would have earned at most 3 sesterces a day, and a legionary 900 sesterces a year. A month's supply of wheat for a single person would cost about 8 sesterces. A knight was required to have property worth 400,000 sesterces, which made him relatively wealthy.

sparsio (pl. *sparsiones*): This word refers to any act of scattering. In the context of the amphitheater, it can mean the scattering of gifts from the *missilia* or the scattering or sprinkling of scented water on the sand and the crowd, to make people cooler and to cover up the smell of blood.

spartor: From the same root as *sparsio*, this word refers to a member of a chariot-racing *familia* who sprinkles water on the horses during a race.

Statius: The poet Publius Papinius Statius (ca. AD 45 - 96) was a younger contemporary of Martial, Pliny, Tacitus, and Suetonius. His shorter poems, called *Silvae* or "building materials," treat a variety of subjects ranging from Saturnalia celebrations to bridge-building; he also wrote epic poetry.

Suetonius: Gaius Suetonius Tranquillus, AD 69-ca. 122, was a friend of Pliny's.

His best-known work is the *Lives of the 12 Caesars*, short biographies of the first dozen Roman emperors. He carefully stops before he gets to the emperor who was alive while he was writing (probably Hadrian). In these sketches, Suetonius usually indicates what games his subject put on, and may tell us something about how the emperor felt about them. The *Lives* are gossipy and rather fun to read, and the Latin is not very difficult.

suppositicius (pl. *suppositicii*): gladiators who fill in for those who are killed during a *munus*.

Tacitus: Cornelius Tacitus lived from about 56-112, dying in the same year as his friend Pliny. He wrote several works of history, covering Rome from the death of Augustus down approximately to his own time. The *Annals* deal with the earlier part of this period and the *History* with the later.

tentor: member of a chariot-racing *familia* who manages the starting-gate.

Terence: Publius Terentius Afer was a playwright who lived from 195 to 159 BC. His six plays, all comedies, were all written in the 160s.

Tertullian: Quintus Septimius Florens Tertullianus, who lived in the second century AD, was a Christian and wrote several theological or moral treatises to teach Christians their faith and to defend it to everyone else. His book *On Spectacles* aims to demonstrate that spectacles are evil and going to watch them is sinful. In the course of this argument, he gives some descriptions of exactly what this evil is and how it came to be.

Thraex: gladiator armed like a warrior from Thrace, with less armor than a Samnite (but full greaves on both legs), a shield, and a sword

tibicen: musician who plays the *tibia*, a woodwind instrument like a recorder

tribune: The tribunes of the plebs were magistrates elected by the plebs (the non-noble citizens) whose main function was to protect the lives and property of the plebs. Military tribunes were high-ranking officers in the army, leaders of the legions.

triumph: an official celebration given to a general for a significant victory over a foreign enemy. Triumphs included processions and often included *ludi*.

Trojan game: a game or performance involving boys or youths on horseback

unctor: one who dispenses oil for gladiators

veles: light-armed gladiators who fight on foot

venatio (pl. *venationes*): hunting, the chase; wild beast hunt staged in the amphitheater, or other spectacle involving animals. A *venator* is a hunter.

Vestal Virgins: a group of six priestesses of Vesta, goddess of the hearth. They served for thirty years, starting when they were girls of six to ten years old, and had to remain virgins during their term of office (though they could be married thereafter).

Virgil: Publius Vergilius Maro (70-19 BC) was the most important epic poet of Rome; his *Aeneid* tells the story of the Trojan hero Aeneas who leaves Troy as it is being destroyed at the end of the Trojan War and comes to Italy to found the city of Rome. Virgil wrote the *Aeneid* and his other poems the *Eclogues* and *Georgics* during the reign of Augustus. He was on friendly terms with Horace and probably also knew Ovid.

Chronology

Some of the earlier dates are traditional or approximate.

753 BC	traditional date of founding of Rome
6th c	Tarquinius Priscus institutes the *Ludi Romani*, Roman games or Great Games
510	Rome becomes a republic
405-396	Rome defeats Etruscans and conquers Veii
390	sack of Rome by Gauls
363	first theatrical *ludi*
264	first gladiator *munus*, for the funeral of Junius Brutus Pera
212	institution of the *Ludi Apollinares*, games for Apollo
204	institution of the *Ludi Megalenses*, games for the Great Mother Goddess
202	institution of the *Ludi Cereri*, games for Ceres
173	institution of the *Ludi Floralia*
44	assassination of Julius Caesar
31	battle of Actium, in which Augustus gains sole power at Rome
17	Augustus celebrates *ludi saeculares*
AD 14	Tiberius becomes emperor
37	Caligula becomes emperor
41	Claudius becomes emperor
54	Nero becomes emperor
68-69	year of the four emperors, ending with Vespasian
79	Titus becomes emperor
80	Titus dedicates Flavian Amphitheater
81	Domitian becomes emperor
96	Nerva becomes emperor
98-117	Trajan emperor
161-180	Marcus Aurelius emperor
204	Septimius Severus and Caracalla celebrate *ludi saeculares*
293-306	Constantine emperor; founds Constantinople and legalizes Christianity
475-476	Romulus Augustulus emperor, traditionally called the last Roman emperor

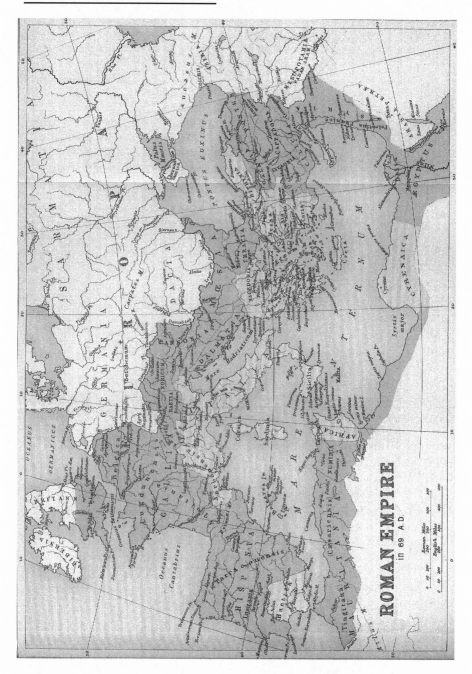

Map 1. the Roman Empire

Map 2. The City of Rome

Further Reading

Ancient sources:

Most of the sources translated here are available in the *Loeb Classical Library*; these translations use the Loeb texts, the Oxford Classical Texts, and occasionally the Bibliotheca Teubneriana. Note in particular ROL = *Remains of Old Latin*, E. H. Warmington.

For inscriptions:

ILS = H. Dessau, *Inscriptiones Latinae Selectae*, Berlin: 1962
CIL = *Corpus Inscriptionum Latinarum*

General references on Roman history:

Boardman, John, Jasper Griffin, Oswyn Murray, eds. *The Oxford History of the Classical World: The Roman World*. Oxford: 1986.
general work describing history, literature, and the arts; illustrated

Scullard, H. H. *From the Gracchi to Nero: A History of Rome 133 BC to AD 68*, fifth edition. London: 1982.
covers the end of the Republic and the beginning of the Empire

On Roman sports and spectacles:

Barton, Carlin A. *The Sorrows of the Ancient Romans: The Gladiator and the Monster*. Princeton: 1993.
describes how the arena reflects the emotional state of the Principate; many untranslated Latin passages

Balsdon, J. P. V. D. *Life and Leisure in Ancient Rome*. London: 1969.
covers work, leisure, and family life, with a long and detailed chapter on public entertainment; many references to primary sources

Cameron, Alan. *Circus Factions: Blues and Greens at Rome and Byzantium*. Oxford: 1976.
standard work on the four colors, with particular emphasis on political developments after the end of the Western Empire

Coleman, Kathleen. M. "Fatal Charades: Roman Executions Staged as Mythological Enactments." *Journal of Roman Studies* 80 (1990), 44-73.
explores why and how the Romans punished criminals in the arena

Hopkins, Keith. *Death and Renewal*. Cambridge: 1983.
four essays, of which the first, "Murderous Games," treats gladiators in the context of Rome as a warrior society; discusses violent entertainment as "safety valve"

Jennison, G. *Animals for Show and Pleasure in Ancient Rome*. Manchester: 1937.
survey by a zoologist with a wide knowledge of the behavior of captive animals

Plass, Paul. *The Game of Death in Ancient Rome: Arena Sport and Political Suicide*. Madison: 1995.
argues that Roman society under the Empire used public violence to control disorder

Potter, David, and D. J. Mattingly, eds. *Life, Death, and Entertainment in the Roman Empire*. Ann Arbor: 1999.
seven essays, two dealing directly with spectacles of all types; lots of references

Scullard, H. H. *Festivals and Ceremonies of the Roman Republic*. Ithaca: 1981.
major work on the Roman calendar, with discussion of when the *ludi* took place and how long they lasted

Wiedemann, Thomas. *Emperors and Gladiators*. London and New York: 1992.
accessible study with many references; argues that gladiator combat was a way for Roman society to come to terms with death

Wistrand, Magnus. *Entertainment and Violence in Ancient Rome*. Göteborg: 1992.
detailed discussion of nine writers of the first century AD and their attitudes toward various forms of entertainment; short but dense

Additional bibliography:
Scanlon, Thomas F. *Greek and Roman Athletics: A Bibliography*. Chicago: 1984.

Index of Sources

See the Glossary for additional information about the authors.

Subject Index